THE NAIL IN THE TREE

THE NAIL
IN THE TREE

*Essays on Art, Violence,
and Childhood*

Carol Ann Davis

T|P

TUPELO PRESS
North Adams, Massachusetts

Library of Congress Catalog-in-Publication data available upon request.
ISBN: 978-1-946482-26-6

First edition: March 2020.

Cover and text designed by Ann Aspell.
Cover art: "The Couple", by Charlie Bluett. 40 x 50 in. Copyright © Charlie Bluett.
Used with permission.

Tupelo Press
P.O. Box 1767, North Adams, Massachusetts 01247
(413) 664–9611 / editor@tupelopress.org / www.tupelopress.org

Tupelo Press is an award-winning independent literary press that publishes fine
fiction, nonfiction, and poetry in books that are a joy to hold as well as read. Tupelo
Press is a registered 501(c)(3) nonprofit organization, and we rely on public support
to carry out our mission of publishing extraordinary work that may be outside the
realm of the large commercial publishers. Financial donations are welcome and
are tax deductible.

 Supported in part by an award from the National Endowment
for the Arts

For Willem & Luke

CONTENTS

A child said, What is the grass? fetching it to me
    with full hands;
How could I answer the child? . . . I do not know
    what it is any more than he.

—WALT WHITMAN

PREFACE

I write this introductory note having just come from stand-
ing watch outside the locked schoolhouse gate as my oldest
son, Willem, now in ninth grade, participates in the Na-
tional School Walkout at Newtown High School, a protest
organized by children at Marjory Stoneman Douglas High
School in recognition of the seventeen educators and class-
mates killed in the latest school shooting to wrack Amer-
ican campuses. Willem was a fourth-grader in Newtown,
Connecticut, attending a neighboring elementary school,
when twenty first-graders and six educators were killed at
Sandy Hook School. After the shooting in Parkland, Florida,
listening to the names read over the radio, he remarked to
me that since he was in elementary school for Sandy Hook
and in ninth grade for Parkland, he really had grown up with
these shootings. *How could I answer the child? I do not know
what it is any more than he.*

I sit writing this at a table at my favorite coffee shop in
Sandy Hook, not three hundred yards from the site of what
remains the most lethal shooting at an elementary school
in the nation's history. This past weekend, in protest of gun
violence, seven thousand pairs of shoes were laid on the

White House lawn to signify the 7,000 children lost to gun violence since that day in Sandy Hook.

I am proud of Willem—who he was before the shooting, who he has become since. I have watched him grow inside this legacy of gun violence, and this morning, first in a video he texted me, then over the police radio broadcasting from the car guarding the school's entrance as the children rallied outside their building, I heard him and his contemporaries chanting *We want change We want change We want change*.

These days I see him transforming himself from a boy asking "What is the grass" into an engaged citizen who will discover and then demand what he needs from a broken world. By the time this collection is published I'm quite sure more shoes will have been placed on the White House lawn. My son and I and his father and younger brother will have marched on Washington, joining thousands in calling for change. Those will be important actions, but so too are the quiet acts of contemplation and utterance each of us perform in reverence to the reality of living here each day.

Willem moves to action now after years of quiet contemplation of the events of his childhood; I complete this book as one impactful period of his life ends and another, his adulthood, begins. But children are wise, perhaps wiser than their adult selves will be. Once during these trying and difficult years after the shooting in our town, Willem explained that the way he felt about the tragedy was similar to a tree with a nail driven into its skin. As the tree grows, the nail becomes a part of it, a gnarled knot in a trunk that nonetheless grows tall and strong. *You would not take out the nail, would you, Mom?* he asked me. *At some point you have to love the nail.* Willem's effort at analogy is the integration of the terrible thing into what he still believes can be a beautiful life.

In the Whitman poem that serves as the epigraph for this collection, the poet goes on to write:

> O I perceive after all so many uttering tongues!
> And I perceive they do not come from the roofs
>   of mouths for nothing.

Not for nothing do we write, paint, love, live, raise our voices in song as well as in protest. These essays are my exercise in practicing what my children have taught me: loving and continuing to love the tree and the nail, the ruin of the current moment and its beauty.

ONE

The One I Get and Other Artifacts •
the day of the shooting, December 14, 2012

> Oil has seeped into
> the margins of the ditch of standing water
>
> and flashes or looks upward brokenly,
> like bits of mirror—no, more blue than that:
> like tatters of the *Morpho* butterfly.
>
> —Elizabeth Bishop

How young were my boys when I moved them to a town, actually not even a town but a hamlet situated inside a town that would, within months, become the site of the largest primary school shooting in the country's history? Luke, five, was sacerdotally young; Willem, nine, was too old not to be told certain things. So the one does not know some things that the other knows too well. The one knows things no child should know. They live together without this mattering much. The older knows when to stop talking, knows how mystery enters through the smallest opening in a conversation about bugs, or which room to sleep in tonight, or toys, and he is vigilant to prevent any darkening wing falling, even momentarily, over his brother. If he can, of course, he will prevent any darkness coming nearer than a penny to an hour.

Within a year or two the youngest will have to be told. It is Luke, the one with no relationship to the events of that day, who will need to be told, though that morning he sat with his father offering the comfortable weight of his living body while his father slowly learned the gravity of the situation: first it was one teacher and she was shot in the ankle, then it was a disgruntled father who shot his wife in a kindergarten classroom, then a survivor under a desk in the office got word out—the first inkling of the blood-cold reality—it was much worse: a first grade classroom, every child.

None of this was exactly true. It was two first-grade classrooms. It was *every child but one*. It was *several who huddled behind the teacher who shielded them*. It was *several escaping by him as he reloaded*. And the children, understanding better than we, are said to have whispered along a long line one to the other by way of explanation *wild animal wild animal wild animal*. Hand on shoulder on hand on shoulder as they were escorted out of the school past the bodies, helicopters already wub-wubbing over their heads in a way that would come to feel oppressive, police-state-ish—under such circumstances *wild animal* was their understanding.

᠅

Luke is sacerdotally young in that he has taken a vow of devotion to early childhood, in that he wears its vestments, cape and sword, and carries its scepter—a juice-box straw. He will have to be told about the tragedy because he will follow this first-grade class with its twenty forced absences through all his years of school. Not now but soon the first-grade class will go to second grade and he will go to first grade. He will sit in its desks and drink its water, not now but soon to be confronted with the real of what had been imaginary. After a kindergarten lockdown drill a month later he told me, *It wasn't real. Real would be someone coming in with a gun.*

And this is what it is *not* to suffer. This is the not-suffering, happy-ending story.

꠸

Recollection is not a perfect machine, as the body is an imperfect keeper of artifacts, but somewhere in my body, in my teeth perhaps, is recorded the following: I am interrupted during my university class by the wild eyes of my department secretary, who beckons me into the hall and says all schools in my town are on lockdown. Ninety seconds pass—not that long, less than a minute—before it is clear to me that Hawley School is not the site of the shooting, but Sandy Hook, a school closer to our house but by an accident of zoning not my children's school. I go back into the classroom without knees and elbows, without joints of any kind. Minus them it is all I can do to make myself sit up-right. I am forty minutes away by car and it is all I can do to sit upright enough to tell my students, end early, go and sit in my quiet office to collect my things—the things of *before* that will come with me to *after*.

Also engraved somewhere, another bodily artifact: a text from my husband, not wanting to cause alarm, reads *I don't know if you're in class but there was a shooting here. Not Hawley School. Luke is home with me. Afternoon K cancelled.*

And this: the principal of Hawley School, in a voicemail to parents a few minutes later, as quietly as she can while still being emphatic, says: *Please hear me: nothing has happened at Hawley School. I have opened every door and seen your children.*

And later my brother, once the news is on CNN, calls to ask: *Do you have Willem with you?* To which I say: *I told you it wasn't our school.* To which he says again: *Do you have Willem with you? I need to know he's with you.* To which I say: *He is.*

And this is what it is *not* to suffer that day. This is the not-suffering, happy-ending story.

⁂

Sacerdos, from the French and earlier from the Latin, literally meaning "offerer of sacrifices." The children who live here, perhaps it's strange to say, now glow. They do, they glow. Everyone can see it. No one can approach unmoved, and the children, understanding their role, shoulder, take on, burden themselves with us. Their skin nearly translucent, they walk around like that, glowing. They offer themselves *like bits of mirror*, and we accept.

We adults take their hands to cross streets, high five when goals are scored or just attempted, correct minor pronunciation errors so that they speak clearly, so that they will be better understood. Words they've read silently, foreign on the tongue, they now say. *Choffer* for *chauffeur*. So we explain: that's from the French; *a* and *u* make an *o* sound, the *ch* is *sh*, and so on.

⚬

Mine were not born here. Mine were born in Charleston, South Carolina. Until last year, they went to schools named for plantations, ate church-revival food, meat-and-threes, corrected those who said lima beans. *No*, they said, *it's butter…butter beans*. Mine loved their Brown House, which they named themselves, loved the near-dark walk to the pool, loved Jack's Cosmic Dogs and the beach, the half hour it took across the Stono River causeway and River Road to get there.

But they are adaptable, easy with burdens. Now they love the snow. They love snow days. They love Blue House and pledge never to move, though we're renting and can't afford to buy. And now they see that lightning bugs appear in more than children's books, that hills can be a part of a yard. Their father has hung an old-fashioned plank swing up between two trees on a hill, so that to swing forward is to fall and be caught by the certain rope, by an enduring constancy. Even *after*, they trust the certainty of being caught.

Into the spring months of *after* my oldest writes a poem that says *Our super power is staying together.*

Has *together* changed for him in a few short months? Which bad thing changed it? There were so many in a row, they were hard to count up and think through. Happening upon us here you might wonder if one can witness such suffering and not suffer oneself.

No, more blue than that. Like tatters . . .

❧

In Central Park, a standoff: you will wear your coats. You will wear them and you will stay near us. But they both run off ahead as if they own the place. This is weeks afterward—how are they not scared *all the time*? But that's us, not them. It's we who look upward brokenly, not them. We forget we are the scared ones twenty times a day, and not before we have said with too much force: *You will stay near me. You will.*

Like trying to catch water in your hands.

❧

I know what it took to put Willem on the bus the first day after, but what did it take to get onto that bus? The most normal act in the world: walk three houses up, wait for the bus. Hear its big brakes, its idling engine, watch it stop. Wait for the door to slide open and step the three steps up.

That was a Tuesday after it happened on a Friday. Later Willem's teacher would tell me the busses' arrival that day was, for her, the scariest moment. What would they find when the busses opened? Who would come? They stood outside, every one of the staff, to welcome mostly full busses back to Hawley School where *Nothing has happened*.

Please hear me.

Google "Hawley School" and you will see pictures of those busses pulling in that day, courtesy of CNN: moon-faced smilers peering out the back of the bus, as on any bus in the country. But it wasn't any bus, it was #8, Willem's. What seat was he in that day? His usual, third from the back, though I know it not from pictures. It stays with me, a compulsive counting of rows to his usual seat. After the bus left our street, I couldn't stop myself from driving to the grocery store parking lot across from the school and counting windows to find his classroom. Top right, facing Church Hill Road. A bank of four windows facing a road momentarily *not* lit with sirens, *not yet* carrying mourners to or from the churches. And busses tucked away at their midmorning idle.

I have opened every door and seen your children.

—⟡—

With the boys that day in Central Park it is early spring—windy, sunny, not warm enough without a coat.

Earlier, the butterfly room at the museum had seemed full of sleepy blue *Morphos* loping along on wingspan alone. The big kids in the room, Willem called them, using his own cosmology. But smaller, less colorful ones fly everywhere, too. The room is humid, tropical, and the volunteers make a parlor trick of walking around with Luna moths on the rims of their ears and hats. I spend more time than I should trying to get a shot of Luke in profile with a Monarch flying by, and then try just experiencing the Monarch flying by the straw-headed, breathing loveliness of him. I put my camera down. Willem gets wind of me, common enough to him by now this peculiar stillness combined with a sudden gravity, but is it too farfetched to say he grabs it off me, tries on its weight? I don't want it to, but the thing in the air that flashes brokenly also belongs to him. He doesn't say anything. He too likes the look of his brother here.

Luke stands very still because he is enjoying the sensation of a wing flying so close to his ear. I am saying to myself, *Benign near-flying thing. Benign near-flying thing, fly on by.*

＊

I understand what that day was like for Luke, at home with his father when afternoon kindergarten was cancelled, and I understand what it was for me, a numbing ride toward Hawley with nothing but Willem on my mind: countryside numb, barns numb, Dunkin Donuts sign numb, cumulonimbus numb, sunlight numb, stoplight-stop-sign numb. All those calls to family to say the boys were okay—brain-wracking calls, who to call next, who will worry—and each call met with a little less comprehension than the last, everyone getting off the phone with me quick. Social-isolation-numb, and dumb.

This was early, remember; we knew more sooner, though knowing didn't mean helping. And who wants to talk to someone so nonchalantly about such a thing: *There's been a shooting but the boys are at another school. It was one in a million and we were two, we were two in a million.*

꙳

All of that I have, artifacts stored in the blood, in the teeth, but what the day was for Willem I don't have. In my mind he is in his classroom with his teacher behind those windows facing Church Hill Road and he is hearing sirens, too many, going on too long. There is the beginning of the helicopter sound that will grow so familiar. He is unsure where any of the sirens are going, but they don't stop at his school and this is all he needs to know. Soon he is told I'm here to pick him up and he gets his things together and walks toward the office. In my mind it is not the drawn, still look of me at the end of the long hall that traumatizes him, but the sirens he's heard for hours.

But in the weeks that follow he corrects me: *I was in the music room. If it had happened at Hawley I would be right there, the first classroom in the building. It would be me.* Before I can take in that he has already made this calculation coherently enough to form such a sentence, before my breathing returns to normal, he corrects me about something else: *I'm not traumatized. Why are you trying to make me feel something I don't feel?*

※

Why are you trying to make me feel something I don't feel? *No, more blue than that.* Toward precision, but never at it. I can get close but I cannot get *there* to where he is.

He is new here but he is a ready friend, all long hair, shirts worn backward and inside out. *Part of my leadership style*, he says when anyone asks about his fashion. Sometimes his jokes are a little far out, a long way around a short block. He is a boy to be admired; I could not have talked to him at his age.

He has a friend who carries a picture of one of the lost children in his pocket. Willem saying this out loud is weeks in the making. The night he tells me, we are lying in his bed until he falls asleep. I ask what that was like, and he says the picture *looked a lot like Luke.* After which he has a stomachache and can't sleep.

※

I keep him home the next day. Stay close to me. Stay near me, offerer of sacrifices.

To which I say: *He is.* When I answer my brother on the phone on the day of, when I say that Willem is with me, it is because I have gone to pick him up. Time is strange, but I get there. My spine has knit together. I have left the university classroom where I teach, I have spent I don't know how many seconds sitting in my office chair in what feels like an air-amber solution, and I have driven the forty minutes home to Newtown. *Home. To. Newtown.* We are new here, but now we're committed.

Please hear me. I have opened every door and seen your children.

To which I say: *He is.*

He is with me because I have stood in the lobby of his school—a lobby that will come to resemble the inside of a pillow, full of hand-made snowflakes and well-meaning notes of consolation—while someone is sent to bring Willem down the long hall from the room on the second floor—the room of sirens, I call it now in mind-privacy, the church of nine years old an echo chamber of helicopter blades—and we have driven home together. It's on this drive that I first notice the glowing; I count the fingers of his hands, hold his left with my right, drive with the other. On the way, on the sun-filled twisty turns of Schoolhouse Hill Road, I've told him in quick, short sentences what's happened and he has said he understands. He has said, *I still feel safe.* He has said, *Let's go home to Dad and Luke. We should be together.* As he utters these sentences I am grateful for the steering wheel. Without moving my hand from his lap I one-hand the hairpin uphill onto Walnut Tree Hill Road and we are *almost home.*

Please hear me. I have opened every door and seen . . .

In the pictures from that day in January a few weeks later, the butterfly's a dark blur near Luke's ear, going too fast for its orange to show, as vestments are sometimes close-held to the body. Or it's not there at all, as vestments sometimes disintegrate into nakedness, as vows are effaced if too lightly held. Luke holds his breath for the interval it takes the thing to pass, then breathes in big, deep breaths. It has passed so close he has heard it. He breathes his living-boy breaths into this early-childhood air, soon gone. It was a dark wing; it passed quickly. And it was benign.

And this is what it is not to suffer. This is the not-suffering, happy-ending story, the one I get.

Before I Get to My Desk •

two years after

Miklós Radnóti, Hélène Cixous

Before getting to my desk this morning I've woken to the back of Luke's spine in blue light and understood for the first time that is the image I have been dreaming of after working the "I" entirely out of a poem that had nothing to do with me and everything to do with the cataract over a saint's eye as Fra Angelico finished painting it in fresco five hundred years ago, everything to do with what, if anything, an angel could tell Mary about what she's getting into when the angel comes with news she'll bear the child of God.

There's some blue light involved, a bent and sleeping spine, some lucky rainfall on the day of his birth.

Before getting to my desk this morning I have crafted a paper grocery bag—thank goodness paper grocery bags still exist!—into a costume for Luke for school, fastening it with *butterfly clips*. What are *those*? He asked when I said the two unexpected words together. Restore me to the wonder of anything named. *What love*? Hélène Cixous might say, as she did when she wrote of Rembrandt in her essay collection

15

Stigmata, a book I return to habitually this year as I return to blue light. When I showed Luke the clip's shape was *like a butterfly* rather than explaining it is just a metal clasp that opens between thumb and forefinger, he nodded his understanding. I suggested we use them rather than taping so that the bag could be easily removed for sitting, for reading, for recess. He agreed. Then I cut from the bottom plastic sheeting of a reusable grocery bag (the kind that stand straight up using this sturdy plastic on the bottom) one round nose and two droopy triangular ears. I taped all three to the face and sideburn area and stood at the bus stop explaining he was *Stick Dog*, a semi-obscure cartoon character some children know and some don't. Cixous again, writing, *it's about our captivity*, reminds me most of what we do for each other, most of what we cut, glean, and shape to wear hides from us our essential fear long enough to bathe us in a captive beauty.

Before getting to my desk this morning I read a poem by the Hungarian Miklós Radnóti, who died in a ditch while performing forced labor during World War II but whose notebook of poems was found upon his exhumation in the raincoat that covered his body. One of his poems reminds me what to do, despite anxiety that feels like a wandering, ambient pain: "pain that wanders around / but you start again as if you had wings." The notebook nestled in consolation next to his dead body for over a year before it was found.

Before I get to my desk this morning my window has reminded me with its frame of the contrasts of a Mark

Rothko painting available in nature's browns and blues, and my dreams have been filled with the strange creatures that inhabit the canvases of Arshile Gorky, especially those with names like *Tracking Down Guiltless Doves*. Who, what hunter, tracks down guiltless doves, I think before I can stop myself. *Start again as if you had wings*, Miklós reminds me.

Before my desk calls, the purple irises have sprung up, lovely weeds that must have something tasteless at their heart, for the deer have left them. And the flowering pear tree that snowed petals down on us all last week as we went from the car to the house to the car to the house, to soccer, to baseball, to band, and back again—that flowering pear readies itself to rain pollen next.

Before I get to my desk a bird of the same type that is dead near our tiny fish pond has visited the dead one's body. *Don't talk about it*, Willem says—all of eleven, the older worried his younger brother will notice, as he notes he must remember his trombone today or miss the performance. *Don't show him. It's too sad.* Later Stick Dog will pass by without seeing.

When Willem shows this level of consideration for his brother, I hold myself back from telling him the story someone told me about poet Robert Desnos saving a whole train car of Jewish persons from the Holocaust, inspiring each of them to recite a poem aloud to him until the guard could no longer see them as the guard had been trained to—as inhuman—but as fulfilling this fundamental human function of reciting words even unto what is surely oblivion. Could they be shot after such an act, though the ditch called to them? These were saved, but Miklós's widow had a book, not a man, afterwards.

Here is Miklós again: *All this could happen! The moon is so round today! / Don't walk past me, friend.* I save these stories for a day Willem can hear them, but when is that day?

Soon, I fear—or worse, the day has already passed. In a way I would not have picked for him, another story has already been told to him, one seemingly ahistorical yet closer to home. In the very town in which we live, Sandy Hook, Connecticut, twenty children and six educators are murdered in their classrooms. Writing it has become a kind of practice, but speaking it is still unnatural, to him or anyone, but especially to him. Should I begin to tell him about Desnos, he might ask me what this has to do with that. And what would I say?

At my desk I wonder how Stick Dog is faring in *his* classroom. Perhaps the best moment of my life passed this morning when I held the two tines of the butterfly clip in my hand above his small back, one hand on his neck, him saying *a little tighter, a little looser.*

Start again as if you had wings. Yes.

How do essays and poems talk to each other over so many answerless silences, and through and past the very events that threaten to (and sometimes do) murder their speakers? Can one art sing to another as I did in my pew those years ago as a child, a call and response rooted in marrow and bone? The essay tells me (from the Latin) to *try.*

The poem says *sing, make.* What would a trying song be? A making try? Making my days in this stunned and beautiful town, I can't help but see that we are with and of the arrow that pierces us.

I think of Cixous, writing forcefully of Rembrandt's slaughtered ox, posing crucial questions about the making of art. Our posture in relationship to the suffering of others, the transience and in some ways the amorality, of beauty: these are her themes. For her, viewing is an act of love, though the "truth" of what we see remains necessarily ephemeral:

Who are we contemplating? Samson's truth,
or Rembrandt's. The blind, the freed, the powerful
slaughtered. The gazed upon. Who by their magnificent helplessness fills us with wonder.
The Vanquished sparkles. (Vanquished but Strong)
Nothing less 'realistic.' To paint this. With what
admiration. What love.

Would Cixous have me *make* something? Would she enact in me another historical slaughter? If I've learned nothing else these few years in this small town struck by sudden violence, I've seen that all is slaughter and prayer, and yet before I get to my desk the world is opening—why go to a desk at all? *All this could happen!* Miklós whispers to me, looking up from his shovel, touching the pocket where the poem is stored, is safe. *The moon is so round today!*

The Practice of School Busses and
Hummingbirds • *in the year that comes after*

RUMI, LARRY LEVIS, IVAN BUNIN

Practice

I am being led. At many moments in the year that comes
after it has been helpful to repeat these four words, man-
tra-style, so as to call a path into being. This being-led has
something of the surrender of sleep combined with an
awareness of self, a self-wakefulness. The result is the blind-
ness of the easily led. I have to relearn each time this part:
don't ask where to or you aren't worthy anymore of the
grand gesture the practice offers you.

Such time as I spend sleeping is time tilted toward sur-
render. In dreams as nowhere else am I being led: some-
times through a window, out into the many-mouthed uni-
verse, or into memory, where a stranger takes my hand and
leads me back to the bleachers at the little-league game from
her car where I've mistakenly gone to wait for my family. I
have told my mother I am going back to the car and she has
pointed vaguely in the car's direction and I have gotten into

a car which looks vaguely like ours and after an interval in which Vishnu's mouth of the universe swallows me I have been discovered in another car, not mine, and spit out again to join my family.

Another Eye

But for a moment, another set of eyes on the scene: imagine walking up to your car and seeing a small girl inside. Such grave responsibility, such a slipping of the known. Surely she is disoriented, she will need the truth plainly spoken, some kind of explanation so that she will come, but this is not exactly the case with this particular girl. The girl I was will go with anyone because—everyone in my family uses the same word—I am gullible. My father puts it more kindly. I can hear him from a distance of forty years: *you are easily led.*

It starts filial, the kind of family story that brands, limits and delimits one, but over time it becomes a practice, something I am happy to claim. Is it too far fetched to surmise I become a poet because of my family's mild rebuke?

Easily led? Yes, well. Whatever else writing becomes, it begins with a willingness to be led.

By now I have learned just how much of my writing life I have spent learning to trust being led, how difficult it is sometimes to obey the physics of the unknown. Imperfect though my practice has been, when the practice leads me back to that moment in the car, I know I've come for some reason. A mini-teleology must exist inside that moment, though I cannot say what exactly it leads to (or even towards), except that the subject of how children read their immediate surroundings is newly important to me. In this story, the one in which I am discovered having wandered into a stranger's empty car at my brother's little league game, nothing sinister happens, beyond perhaps my learning an important lesson backwards: lose and you shall seek.

Not Too Expensive, Not Too Spent

Something to help tease out seeking from being led, a story, because stories are a temporary balm on the lost feeling one has while being led: at the plant nursery where my boys and I are looking for the perfect hummingbird plant that will be not-too-expensive and whose blooms are not too spent for our wild hummingbird visitor to enjoy through the last weeks of summer, we are walking the greenhouse aisles a long time. We pass everything we don't want. One boy is tired, the other rapturous, then the other is tired and the first has a second wind. One pulls me ahead, one back where we've been. I go wherever the force is greatest. They had a nanny they both fondly remember who worked at a nursery much like this one, and we would go and find her and buy plants from her just to say hello. That was a world ago, in another city where plants died if they were not watered on the quarter hour and we had enough money not to hunt like we do now for nearly-finished firebirds, half-hearted salvias, bruised black-and-blues.

We walk a long time in this nursery in a town one town over from our led-to town, and the ground is damp because here too there is someone paid by the hour to water water water. And it is by this route that we come to the already dead and starting-to-wilt swallowtail, yellow and black on the pavement. Suddenly at our feet a worn out treasure, singular in its beauty. I look up from seeing it and find, of course I do, the trumpet flower, red to match the tip of our cobalt bottle-feeder at home for which it is destined to become a late season companion, and we have found the two together. *Found* is the wrong word because it implies a pointed intention or knowledge, whereas we had no idea a swallowtail was anywhere involved in our flower errand. There is no mistaking the feeling we have that *we were led to it*.

At the register the trumpet flower is $2.49 (I even have that much money in my purse!) and the plastic bag for the yellow swallowtail is free. Both come home with us by a series of back roads that I am just learning to our rented home which is ours because we have found it, but found is the wrong word. We are here because we have been coming here for a long time.

Forty Early Mornings

Just months after we get here, a terrible thing happens in our town. Very near us, perhaps a mile through the woods, twenty school children are dead in the space of a few minutes, along with six adults. Surviving parents and siblings live among us, as does a whole school of children who heard or saw what none ever should. We are here for the day, and the aftermath, and the after-aftermath which is the present moment from which I'm writing, all of it new and impossible to comprehend.

Yet I cannot escape what is in my nature to think: that I was led, *easily led* here. I know this without bothering to ask why. The practice of writing has taught me to let the answer travel to me over non-linear distance. Some distances are travelled in language, such as the miles that bring the words of the Sufi poet Rumi. What does Rumi say to my unasked question? "Forty early mornings will do for your gradually growing wholeness." Even Rumi's early mornings this year are painful, home to doubt and rage. And *found* is the wrong word for anything because it implies something of certainty gained. Any wholeness I "find," it's safe to say, may have little in common with certainty. Wholeness itself seems to have left me.

To be led you must surrender, and it's a lesson we learn anew each day here: even the hills, the woods, the rain, and most of all our children sing us toward surrender.

Motorboat-Blank

Such time as I spend at this writing desk is time tilted toward surrender. *Fix your eye on God, and speak not of what you have not seen, that He may implant another eye in your eye.* This is early in a poem of Rumi's (#105), but the advice is very similar to that I tell myself over and over: return to what you see, include nothing you haven't. In practice I broaden the advice to include smell, taste, touch, hear.

Often hearing grows sharp if you close your eyes, or leave them open but draw the mind blank. It's then I'm given the precise sound of the motorboat hidden from me by a line of trees and three blocks of houses down a hillside but as persistent as a lawn mower, on the Housatonic five hundred yards as the crow flies from where I am sitting on my deck. Like birdsong it calls from its moment. Earlier it was the thrumming wing of the hummingbird—sound and touch at once—that wanted my attention.

Two days ago this hummingbird mistook my blanket—bright red in spots, purple in others—for flowers, and hovered, in the way they have, very near me appraising whether pecking my eyes would yield any nectar. Reflexively I closed my eyes, then thought to throw the blanket away from my body.

The motorboat's wub-wub threatens to remind me of the helicopter that hovered that day, the sound of a day that threatens to swallow every sound on every morning of my gradually-growing-wholeness, and I am not sure of the holiness, the wisdom, of allowing such associations. *That He may implant another eye in your eye.*

Another Eye in My Eye

Another eye in my eye. Is that possible? Perhaps *another eye* is preferable to one's own, with the definite surrender of the ego it commands. *I saw it with my own eyes* is a familiar expression. No one says *I saw it with another's eyes*, and yet such empathy is clearly worth striving for. There's something in it akin to that distance novelists talk about needing in order to inhabit a character.

In my small case: I hold a wish to see my children, once, with another's eyes. Not me with theirs, of course. *That* I am not good enough to want. And wasn't each of them, at one time, already another eye in my eye as they heard and felt all I did for the time they were inside my body? On ultrasound film they floated blind, could discern light and dark, heard what I heard, moved with me. When my oldest was born he slept soundest next to me pounding my Royal Deluxe typewriter, a sound from his blind before, a uterine sound, writing a part of his life even then. So intimate a thought it burns to write it.

This image of my son in utero hovers, hummingbird-like, near the subject of the effacement of the individual, the non-attachment Buddhists suggest leads to an end of suffering. And I can accept the idea; I have often said if writing required a vow I would take it. I know if my family required a vow I would take it—do take it, each day. Like the Graeae, three sisters of myth sharing one eye to guard the shield Perseus needs for his quest, I tell myself I would give away my sight for another. I know from the filial story of my sensibility—tilted as it is toward surrender—that I might find some relief in it. To ransom a shared eye and seek from it a common, rather than individual, answer sounds good to me, the youngest of seven children. Writing may not ask so much of me, but love, filial piety, definitely does. My question for Rumi hovers around this effacement of the self, but I have not *found* the question yet. I have not surrendered enough to be led to it.

As I Knew It As a Child

I cannot write what I cannot see, but can I feel what I can't see? Yes, I have learned again this year what I knew as a child. This year has brought back to me how tenuous the world seemed to me as a child, must feel for all children. The many things children know because of what they have seen with their own eyes boggles the mind. Sometimes I catch myself actually happy to hear that some children have blocked what they've seen. In our town we are careful—we have been trained—not to suggest images children may not have seen, images they may have missed. *Speak not of what you have not seen.* We live by this and hope for some mercy, that at least some of them will be shown the mercy of the not seen, will be bathed in a playful blankness rather than end up on the difficult, long road toward (but never at) surrender.

The Graeae

Meanwhile I am being led backwards from the beginning. Looking at my boys I sometimes have the thought: what from my own childhood don't I know? At times, certainly, my siblings and I resembled the Graeae. I find out from research that the Graeae shared not only one eye but also one tooth. I can name each eye and tooth in my family, each blindness or hunger: one sibling who could read the tone of the room, another who had an insatiable appetite, a third with a silver tongue, each of us passing our one gift to the other for filial use, together comprising one whole. My gift: I was small and could hide. Also, I had a photographic memory, and brought back intelligence from my hiding places. Who could use what I offered the group of us? In a family the whole is never totally in view—one passes eye and tooth to someone else and is happily—easily—led by one's pack of Graeae toward what, one never discovers. I simply liked the blind sound of them near me.

Hummingbird Misunderstanding

There is no way to apologize to the hummingbird for our misunderstanding (the blanket is the same color as the new trumpet flower) except to take it and throw it away from my body then close my eyes, which I was practicing not using anyway. At which point the hummingbird understands my deception, my absolute foreignness, and flies away, which I experience as the diminution of wing-beats, the fading of movement and sound.

Has she seen her mistake—gained for a moment an eye that is not her eye—for the interval when the blanket has moved so uncharacteristically, in such an un-flowerlike way? Her hovering displays the admirable quality of curiosity, side benefit and sibling of being led. And she has been rewarded with useless transformation. Seeking a flower she has been given a blanket and a huge creature with two eyes she sees almost too late. Perhaps she feels cheated by the being-led, but it is a spiritual trap, to feel cheated of what one thought one knew. If I could tell her I'd say relish the mistake, but since I haven't fully accepted this yet I can't very well preach it to a flying thing.

Pros and Cons of the Graeae's Photographic Memory

The photographic memory is itself an effacement of the individual: no analysis, just information. There is more room in the memory for information if you are not in the business of assigning meaning. There is also more room for your body to explain memory to you, for your creature wisdom to emerge. And children assign meaning so strangely, anyway. In my town the meaning assigned to the event by the children who witnessed parts of it—no one of them witnessed the whole—was that there was a wild animal loose at their school. From what they understood of the world, it was a probable explanation, and on many levels true. And it's as good an explanation as any.

I Am Set Down Lost

In my research to place our half-torn butterfly not just in its
snack bag but also in its genus and species I find less ambi-
tious butterflies that have elegant, forgettable names. Of a
whole class of *brush-footed butterflies*—do they clean as they
go, like Cinderella?—my favorite is the Eastern Comma,
followed by the Mourning Cloak, and the Tawny Emperor
and the California Sister. I can't think of one favorite with-
out its Graeae clustering around it. In my limited way of
thinking about language I am making something my sib-
lings can share, pass around like a tooth, but the analogy
falls apart on me. Sometimes I am only led so far, and then
I am set down lost. The blanket flies up where I thought I
was looking at a flower and I have to fly hard to avoid being
pulled under. And then there's the problem of hunger, the
hummingbird's reason for seeking me in the first place.

On Boiling

Later in poem #105, Rumi warns about love and also about
interpretation, assigning meanings. He warns that an *eye
asleep that finds no interpretation* will *boil in the love of the One.*
Boiling is such an interesting word, as if love is in danger of
a drowning torture of the worst kind. But what is the One?
Are the things of the earth the One, the danger of boiling in
the love of them a natural enough danger? All too common
and, I worry, filial, this boiling love. I can't ask Rumi if he

means that the love of one's family, left without interpretation, can ruin one. Not to mention boiling grief.

The Eye Asleep

There were years as a child I felt unwatched, not worthy of interpretation, as is probably clear from the little league mistaken car story. But a more pointed example is this: I stayed blindly hungry for twenty years, though I only noticed it when I got to be about twelve, and then starved intentionally for another eight years until something non-filial jogged me out of it. I woke from it a day someone loaned me some sight that was not, could not be, my own. *That He may implant another eye in your eye.*

I woke from hunger when I put on the shirt of my friend Susan, a slight girl. I admired everything about her, and the shirt was a pale vintage silk ornamented with fans in a Japanese style—we loved vintage stores, we had not yet heard of bedbugs—and as I wore it I realized *I am as small as her, maybe I am smaller.* Boiling in the love of the One, had I but to love another. Yet love is, I worry, not the answer to Rumi's riddle of suffering and deliverance but its obstacle. The *eye of the eye of the soul* seems to have very little to do with love. Love is nothing if not effacement, and effacement is not of itself holy. Where is that wise quiet brother, one among my Graeae, when I need him to tell me what a thing means? And where was he when I was wasting myself like that? Perhaps he had passed our eye to someone else.

Future-Blank

At some point the hummingbirds will get too tired, or cold, to come anymore. Then it will be fall and the children will go back to school. While the children are gone I will think grave thoughts about the hummingbirds, displacing my boiling anxiety about the boys—*Where are they? Is everything all right? Are the windows of the classroom open or closed?*—onto these flying hungry things that I can still see. *Speak not of what you have not seen.* I can see the hummingbirds and imagine their journey will take them not very far to a starving death or I can imagine them headed toward some hard-wired long-term and flower-filled destination. And some will find one fate, some the other. Both things will be true simultaneously and the boys will be at school until they come home. Unless they don't.

Even with such anxieties, it is still a comfort to me that I can be led. I can write one paragraph and then another while the hummingbird and the boat motor come and go as they will, as they are made to. And then am I given the blankness, the not seeing. In this way I make it through the hours I am not with my boys, the hours when they are elsewhere, something I can't see.

Invisibility

My boys have gotten into swimsuits and gone with their father to the pool. For the time they are away no interpretation brings them nearer, and I know—because there is no one in my town who has not learned this lesson the hard way—that they could easily be gone permanently. Still, I am going to stop writing in a moment and go see what we have for dinner as if to plan for their return were to call them back into being, back from invisibility.

. . . Or as an Animal

That eye is the eye of the eye, nothing unseen or secret escapes from it. Rumi again, making it sound like I need only look to find. But I don't think Rumi is saying that exactly—what can *the eye of the eye* have to do with being led? That's inward—that is an eye inside, and *of*, possessed by itself—and circular: as in love, what owns what is the question. I own nothing that cannot be taken from me. If I am unwilling to say this, how can I be led? How can I write anything or hope to write?

Poet Larry Levis in *The Gazer Within* gives advice to writers, advice handed down to him in a long line of eye-tooth-transactions over many years. His advice is this: write about yourself from an earlier time, or as an animal.

I have been an animal, I have growled while I waited for news of my sons six months after the terrible thing has happened, while Hawley School went on lockdown for what was, at first, an unknown reason.

A *crank call*, the superintendent of schools calls it later in the voice mail explaining that Hawley School experienced a gun threat related to the events of December 14, 2012, and went on lockdown until it could be determined to be just that, a baseless threat. He is sorry that for some it was an hour before we knew for sure it was only a crank call to the school, especially considering *the year we've had*. He continues on with news of *building hardening projects*, especially at *entry points*.

Right, Rumi?

Nothing unseen or secret escapes from it. Rumi, Larry: I am sorry, I am not an animal but a sieve. The deer's footstep in the woods passes through me, a hummingbird's wing beats through me, the school bus tire crosses over my mind's heart, the handmade cross and the torn wing of the eye of the butterfly and a thousand gone things glance their way toward my boiling. I know it's the time for young deer to lose sight of their mothers. I know the hummingbirds are in their last few weeks before a mysterious fate awaits them, not so different from mine, or my boys', though with my eye of the eye and none other on Graeae-loan, I can't see that clearly.

But it's all okay because I am being led. Right, Rumi?

Animal Wildness

Out on the water the motorboat I can hear but not see is circling, carrying some kids on an inner tube over and over their own wake. At intervals when they fly into the air they shout *hey* and my young deer take note of it, dutifully stop and *interpret* the dream of that kind of repetition, then, led by their hunger, move deeper where we no longer mow. Into the territory we've given over to their animal wildness.

Sometimes You Oversleep

There's an Ivan Bunin story in which a great estate falls into disrepair and is given back to the land from which it came. Storms in the piazza, wind through unfastened windows onto blue tile. Better than any writer, nature is the original practitioner of non-attachment. Not a human scale, not the human eye that judges and interprets, but something else. No *love of the One* to distract nature, to boil the mind, and no filial piety to bind it.

Bunin in his animal wildness writes rapturously about the scent of the apples. The passage begins with being led: *The early days of a lovely autumn come back to me.* Like an animal he is guided by scent. He has not exactly wanted memory's return, but accepts all that comes with its scent. Something from the past, his animal self, moves nearer him. Another line, from the same story: *sometimes it happens that you oversleep and miss the hunt.* A truer line about practice has never been written.

Bus Stop Surrender

Another act of surrender, the most mundane of them all: putting a child on a bus. No matter the child's age, no matter the repetition of the event that is supposed to, like my deer hearing the speedboat, acclimate the danger, it's harrowing. I was relieved to read a whole editorial in the local paper on the subject of school bus surrender right after I wrote the phrase myself, a phrase I realize I've been working up to facing. The editor of the paper must have seen us standing there, little groups of us waiting for the busses, or groups of us watching as the bus heads down the road. Or he's felt it himself. He'd gone to his desk and written: "Tuesday morning, as children headed out to the bus stops, this small 'letting go' for the coming school year may have, for many, proved to be a most difficult moment of surrender."

As Luke—my youngest—left for the pool with his father, I could not stop myself from saying *Jump directly out from the diving board*. Swimming is so new to him he jumps toward the wall so as to reduce the distance he will have to swim. He has not figured out that he can swim and breathe, swim and breathe for long distances. And he has not seen someone smack their head on a diving board and drown. Tragedy is not so far a ready point of reference for him. And it's not one I give him, either, as children are suggestible.

The Hummingbird's Long Swim

Imagine yourself from an earlier time, or as an animal. I can do both at once since I grew up on the edge of the continent and swam every day, great distances I would never allow my own children to swim. But in my own childhood I was unobserved, largely invisible—that much must be clear.

Regularly as early as seven or eight, but at least by the age of ten, I would find myself far out, so far I could look back toward the beach and see the curve of the earth, the beach replaced by an infinity-pool-style water line. Sometimes I swam face first into schools of fish going in the opposite direction. Closer in but still deep, forty or fifty feet of water below me, I hovered on the white fiberglass end of my brother's surfboard—*Graeae, lend me your tooth*—to catch my breath.

The action on the tip of the board is all rear force. I recognize it from the hummingbird at the feeder, though I don't eat as they do at the feeder but drink in the sensation of my brother's attention. My feet move unseen underwater. While this is happening I am occupying the line between starvation and non-starvation as hummingbirds perpetually must. Swimming is part of the starving. Keep moving, spend more energy than you take in. Mine was a hummingbird's economy, and like the hummingbird it is my weakness that is fed when I look at my brother, one hand casually on the tip of his board.

Did I spend those tender years a few heartbeats from collapse or is it simply a child's reality to feel it so?

Arguments at the Continental Shelf

Make tearful the eye of the soul at every moment, Rumi says, warning of *human stature and cheek*. I struggle with whether for me my boys are part *human stature and cheek* or part *eye of the soul.* Am I to attach to them or accept that they are part of my own ego, my self-struggle, and create a distance from which to observe them outside of myself?

I am an animal when they are not yet returned to me, this is all I know, but not the kind of animal I was out on the ocean. Then I was young and starving, driven. Now I am a wounded growl. I am pushed beyond anything I can know, and being led, for the first time in my life, is poor consolation, regardless of what writing gets done.

In this diminished state, at the diminishment of the bus stop, I am ready to argue everything with Rumi. *At every moment* is too tall an order. It requires too much devotion, a ridiculous degree of being led. Rather than passing an eye or a tooth, this requires total surrender, Abraham and Isaac style, on the mountaintop. I am not with my boys most of the time. God tells me being with them is like gorging myself on a meal; it is gluttonous. Rumi, the eye of the eye of the soul is theirs, not mine. No Graeae keeps the eye too long in its own possession. There is an unbridgeable distance, an unfathomable depth, between them and me, the shelf of a continent. I close my hollow eye-holes not to be pecked to death by the fact of it.

Taken, Not Taken

The curve of the earth is a kind of eyeball I've swum inside, a floater on the pool of the eye of the world. Why should my boys be any less vulnerable than I was?

The trees are already thinning. The mornings are cool. Like water down the drain we are taken as we are being led. Often when I think of the children in my town I use that word, taken. This one. *Taken*. And that one, *not taken*. But I have not written that before. It seems wrong even to make such a distinction and worse to confess it.

The Hummingbird's Forgiveness

While I'm writing this word, *taken*, the hummingbird comes up to me, close again, as if having forgiven my transgression. Upstairs the school supplies are stacked, boxed. In one of my boy's backpacks, the yellow swallowtail—the Eastern Tiger Swallowtail to be precise, female because of the blue on back of wings—is packed up to show to his new class. If it is not injured by the bus ride, or if he doesn't take it out during the curvy windey ride and drop it, and all the other ifs I will never really comprehend, much less see with my eyes. *Speak not of what you have not seen.* Because I am trying to practice Rumi's dictum I don't say more. I can't see all the ifs; like the universe, they're expanding invisibly far around me.

Winter Apples

All that's left is simple surrender. Everyone agrees from Rumi to Bunin to Levis. The aging Russian estate is a metaphor, the very scent of apples a symbol for the repetitive and perpetual nature of loss. Practice losing, the image commands me. The apples themselves are *Antonovkas*, winter apples, bred for their heartiness. I am literary enough to understand some parable of endurance, but I am also an animal. I understand the starving dive toward a foreign thing, and the eye's quick close, the rejection of the probable. And I am exhausted, already starving. I cannot let my boys go—can I?—should I be asked to. But of course if they're taken I won't be asked. *Everywhere the secret of God is coming*, says Rumi. And it's terrifying, no?

I am always with my boys or about to be with them or leaving them or they are leaving me. This is my very mundane problem, the line filial between hunger and starving, finding and being led.

Rumi, lend it to me, the tooth, the eye. Ransom it for a shield, a certainty, but then I'd be on a quest, and being led is the opposite of a quest.

My Graeae Plays Ball

While my brother plays his little league game and my father coaches and my mother looks on in the bleachers, I sit quietly in the car. I think how many things in this car I don't recognize, but believe as only a child can that I have simply not noticed them before. The foreignness of the situation eludes me, or pleases me. By nothing but my own imagination am I led into a story that includes my mother going to the store, my mother picking up Kleenex for the car, buying a little organizer caddy for the "hump" in a big American car of the kind you rarely see these days. Or on some level I know this is not my own car and am not alarmed. The crowd calls familiarly from the game, and I wonder in my eye-toothy way whether it is my Graeae or someone else's who has made the winning play.

And then the owner of the car comes back. Out of foreignness and back into the known world am I led.

Into Coming Dark

Before the owner of the car came the sense was inside me that anything could happen; a foreignness, my own, was not asleep but wakeful. Though I felt connected to my parents, to my Graeae on the field, I was also happily blind, momentarily without an eye to see them, unable to look *for* anything. And this is the part of being led that is so different from searching. What one finds when one searches one has set out looking for, but one doesn't even know when one is being led or toward what. Like childhood it is a blind journey. Frames of reference fall away.

Rumi addresses this and—I have to believe—children know it, too. Inside all of Rumi's warnings, he offers a respite: *Eye asleep and yourself wakeful—such a sleep is perfection and rectitude.*

Perhaps the practice of the school bus is this, *eye asleep and self wakeful.* Perhaps the practice of letting the taken be taken and the not taken not taken is this, *eye asleep and self wakeful.*

I can't go on my boys' blind journeys. Mostly I have

to stay back. The known slips out of its clothes, out of the
house, out of the body, down the street and into the air. It
slips from the feeder into the just-thinning trees, into the
coming dark. I can't follow, or search for anything certain.
I can only be led.

Memoir of Sleep and Waking •

two years after

Eva Hesse

> I would like my work to be non-work. This means that
> it would find its way beyond my preconceptions.
>
> — *Eva Hesse, on her installation* Chain Polymers

At three a.m. the world is sound only, dark sheets of breath. *Chaos can be structured as non-chaos.* Eva Hesse told this to someone at *LIFE* magazine the year she died. It's quoted in a museum catalog that also contains *evchen's first yom tov,* part of a family scrapbook mashed up inside a critical essay along with Hesse's adamantine late comments on doing art wrong, letting it misbehave. Two scrapbooks have survived the modern shipwrecks of kinder-transport, emigration, a life in Washington Heights in which Hesse's mother stepped off the roof of a building without a word when Eva was ten.

At three a.m. there's the plainness of one's isolation, a trapped quality of the body. My youngest boy, once through the night terrors that visit him forty minutes after he first closes his eyes, rests at my side like a clock. Listening to him I remind myself that everything ticks like a machine when a child. Perhaps it's this ticking that started the mechanical in Eva's work, the repetitious, obsessive explorations that became sites of crucial "wrongness" and discovery, causing her to seek the *non-non*, not-work, *beyond my preconceptions*. I can see how that would be, the morphing of materials into an enduring thought-machine, a world of dripping, insoluble questions posed by poured latex and fiberglass. Some pieces were only ever precisely installed in-studio, others left untitled for intervals on their way to names that accommodated their own inherent and illogical unknowns: *Sans II*, *Aught*, *Contingent*, *Repetition Nineteen*, each leaving opaque the undrawn connections between biography, thought, and practice. But precision played a role, too: her notebooks contain long lists of synonyms, each alternate worked over until a title was deliberately assigned.

My boy wakes repeating *I don't know I don't know*, unsticking himself from the insoluble problem of the dream. I would explain to him about structuring chaos, but after a minute he is awake enough to see me, says *okay okay okay* and falls back onto the pillow as if he has been shot. In the Germany Eva left at two, a Germany almost before memory, she recalled night terrors, a bed with brass bars at the foot, her father coming in to assure her *no one will rob us, no one is coming for us*.

> What I want of my art I can eventually find. The work
> must go beyond this.
>
> — *Eva Hesse, on* Chain Polymers

I had meant to begin this essay with the bus that comes for
my two boys in sequence every morning and returns them
every afternoon, but I have not yet found what this has to do
with Eva Hesse, who had no children and died at thirty-four
of a brain tumor. I had wanted to discuss process, Eva's re-
petitive shapes similar to my own obsessive columnar linea-
tion, a form that seems to trap my poems and has done so for
years as I work out what it has to tell me. In this my process
resembles Eva's habit of sending the work beyond what she
can find through exploration of material. Language can ap-
proximate a fiberglass sheet laid over its subject—as it dries
becoming brittle enough to break itself on what it knows.
What I want of my art is not at all what will come out of it.

The great coincidence of one's process meeting the
machine and material of its making—this is an appealing
idea for anyone in the uncertain process of composition.
My work with poetic language as material both organic and
inorganic attempts to rattle it toward *beyond*, past *what I can
eventually find*. Underpinning the drying material of words
on the page, behind all and ever *in* my work (subject and
medium): the machine of my boys' coming and going has
not broken, not yet. *What I want* versus the work that *must*

go beyond it—as regards my boys—is a problem that does not go unnoticed by me.

Sculptural, their routes ropelike, yellow busses are threading their way everywhere through town right now. I remain at my desk on the implicit assumption those machines get where they're headed. Often during this time in which they are in transit, I open my Rumi and read. Like Eva, Rumi was a fan of obsessive repetition: the Sufis danced in circles until they were visited by prophecy and vision. Today where I open his book, Rumi says *birds, who are now parted from your cage, show your faces and declare where you are.*

Declaring where they are, images of Eva herself litter my desk, photographs taken at different times in her life. Top of stack is Eva in a cane chair by a white window with a white radiator under it, a polished metal dome light facing away and unlit clipped to the chair's cane back. Hair pulled back over one shoulder, everything about her is neater, prettier than her art. At some point she says *nice parallel lines—make me* sick.

꙳

It is my main concern to go beyond what I know and what I can know.

— *Eva Hesse, on* Chain Polymers

Nice parallel lines she gets past very quickly, but parted-from-cage is not a bad way to describe the obvious flown ropes of

Right After, which endures in its museum-ceiling setting as a well-conceived meditation on non-attachment, as well as the frame of her arms flying up in pictures in which her face shows partially through plastics, ropes, and wires, encased if not caged. A very late picture of her taken in the month before her last operation for the brain tumor that will kill her appeared alongside the chaos remark in *LIFE* magazine. Like memory, like dreams, the body shuttles through *what I know and what I can know*. Standing behind rubberized yellow ropes—and these are the last ropes—she looks at the camera. They don't cage or encase so much as ensconce, but the word is wrong. Elsewhere she describes what she wants in her art: *everything, but of another kind, vision, sort*. Was this other *kind* she sought the abidance to a reality imprinted on her earliest consciousness, something she came to call *the absurdity of it all*? She repeats that phrase so often in interviews she finally vows she will no longer say it.

The last picture in the catalog of Willem de Kooning's 2012 MOMA retrospective shows him after all but color and line had left his memory, arms full of starfish, his grey hair lit with sun. An elegy of a photograph, it takes up the back interior cover of the catalog and spills into overleaf. I walked through the rooms of that retrospective chronologically, and was delivered onto the high white shore of his late paintings. It's a sweet return to the sure-handed line of his early sign-painting days, and offers sharp relief to the dissembling, changeable lines Hesse fashioned from latex-draped rope and wire. In the de Kooning picture, his line stays with him in backlit horizon of deep-blue-down, light-blue-above; I look at it and wonder if this straight line would make Hesse sick.

Rumi open at my desk answers: *your ship has stopped on this water, wrecked; like fishes, for one instant rise from this water.* Their late periods differ in many aspects, among them their approaches to the line, but a common ropy certainty inheres in both Hesse and de Kooning, as if each could move and *rise from this water.*

I am not sure what de Kooning's practice was late in his life, but Eva races into her work in the final year, not unlike poet Sylvia Plath's fabled three-month composition of *Ariel.* But because the end will not be outrun, there is a *last rope work*, or, as it is called, *Untitled (Rope Piece), 1970,* the one hanging in her studio at her death. Taken from studio and installed posthumously, like Plath's specific notes on the preferred order for poems in *Ariel,* Hesse's detailed guidance remained in typewritten notes for her friends to follow in their placement of her hooks and wire. Their adherence to her wishes has the emotional weight of de Kooning's picture on the beach; its precise installation—permanently on view at the Whitney—serves as permanent elegy. Hesse advised them:

ropes rubberized with filler all sizes widths colors
connected to plastic one I made but reaching closer
to what I had envisioned for that piece the way it had
started before I got sick. hung irregularly tying knots

as connections really letting it go as it will. Allowing it to determine more the way it completes its self. make it with at least 2 or 3 of us, connecting from wires from ceiling and nails from walls and other ways let it determine more itself. how floppy or stiff it might be. colors. how much rope / must be rope piece.

In the installation her friends did their best in *really letting it go as it will...allowing it to determine more the way it completes its self.* It's clear she expects only to get *closer* to what she envisioned, never to arrive *at* it, chance irregularity leading to what must out from the work itself, and yet from the grave she exerts a certain amount of control, adding the imperative *must be rope piece.* Material certainty doesn't leave her, though she surrenders to the chances it will bend and drip. The question of the line doesn't leave her either: *how much rope.* No real answer to how much but *Non. Sans. Aught.* As it works *irregularly* on itself, the work works itself out, headed beyond what the artist understands.

⚓

The formal principles are understandable and understood.

— *Eva Hesse, on* Chain Polymers

Getting to the point where *formal principles are understandable and understood* is the work of one, even short, lifetime. In an interview, Hesse retrospectively mentions *Hang Up,* a piece she began in a German warehouse where she was surrounded with industrial materials and cast-offs: *I was still using cords and ropes, though about this time I started dropping it and not using it so rigidly.*

Drop it, don't use it so rigidly.

My boys will come home on their busses one after the other. If I have been out I will race down Meeker Hill, up Poverty Hollow, and down Schoolhouse Hill to beat my older boy home. I will find him standing at the locked front door fiddling with a key he hasn't mastered. An hour later my younger boy gets dropped off at a bus stop three houses up from our house.

On the way home he tells me we've passed the darkest day of the year.

On a day Eva's brain is tumor-rich, she collapses before she can name *Expanded Expansion*. For a while until she can get out of the hospital that first time—there will be three operations within a year—and name it, the piece goes by *Untitled*, something that doesn't reflect the care with which it is made. Perhaps because her time runs out on her that non-name name will come to rest forever on the piece her friends install as elegy. And *Untitled* will become the de-facto title of numerous paintings. Or leaving so many pieces untitled is her choice, a response to *the absurdity of it all.*

She is young in every picture because she dies young, but even young there is *early work* and *late work*. There are *art school drawings* and *paintings in the expressionist mode* and *rope work* because she worked so deliberately. She won't ever be

Papa de Kooning with his arms of starfish, partly because the nature of suffering is that it is individuated; he will meet his suffering and she hers without one correlating to the other. Hesse especially understood this, insisting that art was *my life, my feelings, my thoughts*, the formal questions (such as anything can be understandable, understood) secondary to those which remain necessarily outside of understanding.

Before that first trip to the hospital, her mind's a pretty thing piled up with gears and condensation, her body an ocean played backwards. How exactly does a fish rise up out of that water? The body looks for words for infirmity, but *I cannot retrieve it I cannot retrieve it I cannot retrieve it*. At some point she can no longer do the physical work her work requires. The *contingent*, always a part of her process, takes on new meaning, so that this word becomes the title of a significant late work, eight fiberglass sheets hung in the manner of paintings, but at a 90-degree angle to the museum wall. About *Contingent* she would write, *question how and why in putting it together? can it be different each time? why not? how to achieve by not achieving? to make by not making?*

In an interview the year of her death, Eva keeps speaking of all she wants to do *but illness prevented it*. For the first time she uses assistants, and there are questions about whether the work is as it would have been had she effected it herself. Judging by her responses, those questions seem inconsequential to Eva, but reading them in retrospect they border on cruel. Earlier, describing intervals of illness, she'd said *in between it was pretty much hell*. This is perhaps a reason to use rope in one's work, a reason to string things from the ceiling by hooks—as if by representation to admit the prone elements of psyche and physicality. Her habitual manifestations—the being-dismantled and the setting-up-to-be-un-done—survive as honest assertions of the particular way in which material life effaces the individual. All this time later, as fiberglass cracks and decomposes, the work can't be denied its affecting temporality, its reason-for-being actuality, orphaned so long though it has been from its young maker.

Later in the same interview: *The world thought I was a cute, smart kid and I kidded them.*

Speaking of kidding: she put *Aught* and *Augment* in the same show, one strung from the wall, the other coming up from the floor, so that people could think the two were one piece if they didn't read the titles. Yet their titles are etymological cousins. *I kidded them.* At some point she is a kid in a bathtub.

I am probably the only mother in my child-loving town who does not bathe my children regularly, as Evchen was bathed up until the kinder-transport by her mother who was *beautiful and sick.* I could say it's because our water comes from a well and it would be like bathing my children in river water, which is not so bad I guess. At the bus stop—the boys hate this—I can be seen running a moistened finger around a mouth or on the smudged tip of a nose.

After my own bath there are deposits of sediment in the tub from deep underground. Piled behind the toilet are great soiled rags I've used to wipe away this river sludge because I am addicted to what my own mother called *a warming bath.*

These towels stiffen over time into objects. They contain a solidity. It is as if they *think*.

Eva again: *I want to try other possibilities and work more direct.*

⤝

It is the unknown quantity from which and where
I want to go.

— *Eva Hesse, on* Chain Polymers

At some point before they are separated by war Eva is illuminated by candles at a last Sabbath with her parents. Soon after she is two years old and—imagine it—on a train with her sister, five. Then she is too sick to stay with the host family and so is separated even from sister Helen. In the interview before she dies, she says *I have one healthy sister*. At two years old, looking out the hospital window onto a strange city that did not contain her parents, she must have thought, *I have one healthy sister*. From the blank space after she says it in the interview I can tell the interviewer can find no way back from this sandbar to the art, but for Eva there's no difference. Her illness and her history are part of her art. What happens to her happens to it. Art is experience's contingency.

As soon as he can her father begins telling their family history in a diary (still extant). For the first time because he has fled to London from Germany he can write *without the danger of losing my head because of it.*

Even before waking, our weekday mornings begin

with the bus. In pre-dawn light the high school bus takes its dream-pass, atop the hill and gone. An hour later, my eldest son's bus stops at the same spot for him. Our house is in a hollow, so at the front door I can stand unseen and watch him up there, balancing his father's trombone case on its wide mouth, alert to the sound of bus brakes the next stop over and calling to me *I love you have a good day*. Which means *go further out of sight quickly in your torn pajamas*.

Rumi: *Is it that the mold has been broken and rejoined that Friend?*

Eva used columnar molds for *Repetition Nineteen*, no two exactly the same but rather *different each time*. Process is never *not* a walk into the unknown. Dark sheets fall on it, around it, from it, sculptural and structured, illusory and allusory. I move out of sight of the bus because I am asked to. The mold breaks to rejoin the friend. The mold *breaks* to rejoin.

Because language is a concordance of questions, full of exceptions, innuendo, and historical unknowns, children grow by wading through its chaos, register the tick tick of everything around them. Because childhood is holy, its secrets are eventually lost, Dead-Sea-Scroll-inscrutable, untranslatable. Scriptural and sculptural. *Come take your bath!* In scrapbook pictures Eva is a child kept clean up until the day history comes for her.

As a thing, an object, it accedes to its non-logical self.

—*Eva Hesse, on* Chain Polymers

Last week my boys took two friends into the woods and walked a mile down an immigrants' road that runs behind our house. A century ago Irish immigrants took this road into Sandy Hook center—less than a mile from here—to work at New York Belting and Packing, a factory that made fire hoses and rubberized belts. This was shortly after the vulcanizing process made rubber a popular and affordable commercial product. All the qualities Eva describes as appealing to her about rubber—its thinness, its flexibility, its inherent expressive and irregular shapings—made it a major economic driver of the early twentieth century. Hoses will carry water and poison into Eva's world, but before they do, immigrants will walk this path, crossing the stream at Black Bridge.

On this path, my boys walk until they see a tent, and across from the tent, what they describe later as a "sensing device." My older boy calls out *who lives here* and no one answers. They return home right away and tell me their story. In the telling, the story immediately becomes object, acceding to its interiority, its non-logic. Its unknowns glisten as they tell it.

In the interview Eva is asked about the temporariness of art, the fact that many of her fragile materials will likely decompose with age; the interviewer, walking on hot coals, says, *Are you concerned with the idea of lasting?* Eva: *Well, I am confused about that as I am about life.*

Rejoin that to its mold, friend. Hang that from its ceiling.

⚐

It is something, it is nothing.

— *Eva Hesse, on* Chain Polymers

Two years ago in my town there were those who put their children on school busses and never saw those children alive again. Instead of at the bus stop, they stood in a fire station after every living child in the town had been picked up and taken home. Then they were told the unthinkable.

In his diary, Eva's father recalled the morning of his daughters' kinder-transport departure this way: *Then came the sad farewell from the children at the railway station in Altona. Will there be a reunion? Will we be murdered first? We were not allowed on the platform.* He goes on to note that Eva and Helen were accompanied onto the train by the Gestapo.

Eva describes her family's emigration as *very late, the last chance.*

How except in calcium and sleep could such an event accrete inside surviving children? The context into which memory places itself accretes outward from its beginning; encased in the material of the present moment, it seeks its medium.

It is something, it is nothing.

— *Eva Hesse, on* Chain Polymers

Every day Luke climbs the three steps of the bus to a seat by the window where, depending on his mood, he sits where he can see me or where he can't. It is his luxury to look and see his mother or not. He is expert at hiding in his hoodie and last minute cutting his eyes toward or away from me. In the family scrapbook there is a baby picture of Eva's mother alongside the words *Allez Ruth!* And later in the same book her father narrates *loss of possession and profession.* Long after they are both gone, Eva gives names to her work like *Sans* and *Right After* and *Expanding Expansion* and *Hang Up.*

Some days the bus that comes is a different bus, its number 8 pasted with paper onto the window above the bus's real number decaled in boot-black on the side. Invariably these other busses have darker windows, and I look for Luke through a darkness that recalls the bulletproof glass of a president's motorcade. Friend, has it come to that? Friend, it has always been that.

To the interviewer with no shortage of questions that cut to the quick, Eva said something that addressed the beautiful light that surrounds her rope hangings. Explaining about *Right After* that though she is not trying for beauty, light is *part of its anatomy*, she added *maybe dark does beautiful things to it*. Light and dark are both essential to its anatomy.

To separate the two is to be less than direct.

I find Luke's face in the glass, and dark does beautiful things to it.

⤙

It is something, it is nothing.

— *Eva Hesse, on* Chain Polymers

Eva spent an interval of fifteen months in Kettwig an der Ruhr, Germany, in 1964–65, five years before her illness and death. She spent a lot of that time fighting with her husband, shopping, going to museums and openings, reading, and staring out her high studio windows in her industrialist patron's warehouse floor-through. So near her childhood home, she attempted to visit but was turned away by the current tenant-owners; altogether child and adult spent no more than four years in Germany.

The five remaining years of her life in studio in New York glisten with extraordinary work begun in that former textile warehouse littered with disused machines, every drawing and object—really every utterance—locating in Hesse an increasingly emphatic particularity of point of view. At some point she describes her drawings from her time in Kettwig as *clean and clear—but crazy like machines.* Perhaps the mold breaks and rejoins *inside* the mouth of the wolf, given its anatomy of beauty and darkness. *It is something or it is nothing.* Accepting the wedded-together limitations and possibilities of the material she is given, embracing its contingencies, Eva allows her work to shuttle along the border of something-nothing.

There's a story about a shop girl treating Eva badly even though she had the money for the boots she was buying, and a Christmas party where someone bumped her, spilled her drink, tore her dress. All this she noted in a diary that survives, a quarter the size of a kindergarten primer. Under her window, as they had all the days of her life, busses and trams came and went, parting and rejoining as track to wheel is joined.

On Brotherhood and Crucifixion •

two years before

Georgia O'Keeffe, Charles Fletcher Lummis,
Simone Weil

Black Cross, New Mexico, 1929 (Georgia O'Keeffe)

Twin of the one in my mind, this cross is uneven—blooms
like the trunk of a heavy woman, its underside bright as sun-
set, and below it, O'Keeffe's hills—like *looking at two miles of
grey elephants*, she said once—a sort of bed where no cross
lies down. The sky's a kind of vanishing of the arcs, blue
enough for anyone who wants it. The thin sunset trapped
forever under the heavy arms of the cross, sky before sunset
free and foreshortened above, cross and shadow of cross
made one.

*Photograph of a Crucifixion, 1888
(Charles Fletcher Lummis)*

And there we stood facing each other, the crucified and I, says
Lummis of following the *penitentes* brotherhood outside San

Mateo, New Mexico, to the spot chosen to crucify one of their own on Good Friday. This after their self-flagellations all through Lent. Lummis reports that the man *sobbed like a child* when he learned he would be roped rather than nailed to the cross. In Lummis's picture the man's face is covered in black cloth, his body in white, and two brothers steady the cross upright, hold the ropes as mast and sail are held to wind. Taut.

Black Cross Again

O'Keeffe has said she thought the cross she found and painted was left by the *penitentes*: *I saw the crosses so often—and often in the most unexpected places.* Often enough to feel as if a group of men practiced something fluid and secret in her midst, perhaps among them the man who helped her stretch the canvas for her largest picture—*Sky Above Clouds, IV*—not at all secretly but quietly outside her garage. The wood broke easily overnight and in the end she required a stretcher made of steel.

Lummis Again

He was recovering from a stroke, but on Maundy Thursday had invited to table among others the one to be crucified, asking at the end of the night if he could photograph them the next day. At first they acted as if they knew nothing—What ceremony?—but at dawn he was among them when they walked into the hills. Before long the crucified's head rested on a rock. Behind them hills where no cross lies down.

Fishers of Men

Of course it is possible to die on a cross just as it's possible to evaporate entirely into symbol—pain something made of marrow and bone, entirely surrendered to and therefore left on earth. It might be a certain kind of gratitude that compels the man toward the cross, instrument of his undoing. These are things I thought about as a child. I had an overactive imagination and too many church hours to log. I had a long beach at one end of my street, a river at the other, and five brothers, two among them named James and John: the life of an apostle was not so far from my frame of reference. I knew how to bait a hook. One time my brothers decided to fish all night in a camp on an outcropping of rock twenty feet out in the river, and I visited them. They were as primitive and important as apostles, having waded out to the rocks holding their gear above their heads. They squatted there with their poles as I walked home in the supernal light to my parents who let these things happen with a kind of carelessness.

Inside the Morada

Inside the *morada* where the men gather the adobe walls are painted a bright white. In the windows hang curtains or heavy paper. Rough-hewn supports, and enough room for the *hermanos*—lay brothers of the order—to stand facing each other. It's said that they never refuse a request for help—perhaps this is why Lummis was permitted to take his picture. In these quarters they watch each other draw blood. Perhaps here the crucified received the four inch long wound in his side that Lummis reported. It's not visible in the photograph.

Simone Weil calls the moment when Christ calls out on the cross the moment when affliction, human affliction—a suffering of body and soul, combined with social degradation—enters the mystical body of God. This is a great privilege for Him. He has at last crossed the distance between God and God, something only he can do, she tells us, and thinking of this, I wonder if such a distance finally blooms as interior or exterior space, or a third something I'm incapable of understanding but somehow related to perspective in painting. The distance is exterior if it's the distance the *penitentes* walk together from the *morada* to the crucifixion point in the hills, or the distance of *Sky Above Clouds IV* to the ground below (O'Keeffe so afraid of flying she did it only when Alfred Steiglitz lay in a New York hospital and later, only for the view). Or the distance is entirely interior, the one I walk from my writing table to the living room, where my two sons duel first with pillows then with swords; I hear the change in weapon before I see it. Or it's the distance between the swords as they move through space, each swing relative to the other—a third thing that locks them into reticulation with one another.

Point A to Point B

First the *penitentes* drew a line in the sand one hundred feet from the crucifixion site and told Lummis to stay behind it. Then having looked through the viewfinder and seen the picture too small, Lummis asked to move closer and was given another line thirty feet from the man on the cross. This is the vantage point of the photograph.

From here Lummis could clearly hear the man begging: *Not with a rope. Not with rope! Nail me! Nail me!*

Inside the Studio

In my friend Cliff's studio on the campus where we both teach in Charleston, South Carolina, are at least thirty faces on differently sized canvases. Some other paintings, but mostly the face. He has painted exclusively this subject for many years, telling me that each is new and difficult because of the demands of the real. I look at him and think *reckoner*.

I have seen these faces change on him before my eyes. In fact I have seen myself change, the quick motions of his hand covering over my nose and chin and eyes with paint. Then two weeks later, twin portraits of me to choose from—one that looks directly at me and one that might, just this minute, turn away forever. I choose *Reckoner* and he lays her carefully in a cardboard carrying case he's made for me. The portrait choice has called to mind the way in which to reckon with is to be seen by another—sometimes that other is the self (as with my portrait), sometimes it's attention the maker of an object bestows (Cliff to me, Lummis to the brother on the cross, O'Keeffe to the landscape). And sometimes the reckoning is a third thing, unnamed, moving in, out, and among us, as with my boys and the swords.

Next to *Reckoner* wrapped for carriage on the couch, Cliff's guitar. I imagine him at all hours with his fingers on the strings, the two paintings at various stages of making on the walls for the weeks he keeps them, and I have no way of knowing which face turned to look at him at any given moment, but neither has he and for this I am unaccountably consoled. He's told me before that he's the eldest brother and when I think of him those weeks with both paintings I feel the brother portion in him and am grateful in an ancient kind of way.

Brothers

Perhaps it is the idea of a brother to witness your pain that has brought the *penitentes* together. I at least would like to think of witnessing as something holy—certainly Mary did as she stayed with the soldiers throughout the crucifixion of her son. One who loves another would take his pain, and perhaps the crucifixion is just an example of something innate we know from looking across at each other at a space of thirty (or five) feet.

I have seen this wish manifest between my own two sons—the older needing badly to quiet or at least comfort the younger. After two bad accidents the younger weathered in his first year, every time the younger one is remotely hurt the older asks if we should take him *to the hospital*. Having felt at a loss to help his brother twice, my oldest son lives in fear of just that moment. Once awakened, there is no quieting such a fear.

But what if witnessing is a kind of cause? Perhaps without a witness, pain disappears. Solitary, unwatched, O'Keeffe painted all those years the whiteness of bone, a large whiteness that becomes no one looking, that is only ever a thing washed clean by rain. I would surely turn my head if it would cause the abatement of another's pain. Unlike Mary I like to think I would walk away from the cross. *And there we stood facing each other, the crucified and I.*

Blows

My brother Rick remembers standing in front of the younger children (me included) in order to shield us from the unaccountable as it assuaged us in various forms throughout our childhoods, something that even at fifty-two Rick seems to pale when recalling. I cannot remember much of these moments but I believe him; because my love for him can grow feral without my anticipating it I know that I would not be alive without him. Nothing I can do takes back that I was not only witness but cause of his suffering. I cannot escape the feeling that I am here on the earth because of him. This brings me close—*close*—to what the feeling of being a brother must be.

The Nail

Concerning the *divine technique* of the crucifixion, Simone Weil writes that the *infinite distance separating God from the creature is entirely concentrated into one point to pierce the soul at its center.* This is the nail whose head is infinite but whose point is tiny and precise. This is the nail the *penitente* was asking for, but his brothers, because they would have him live, substitute ropes and therefore open the several distances again.

Preparing the Paint

Cliff tells me flecks of mica are mixed in his white. Cobalt is ground into the cobalt paint and these are the paints he has always used. He has to send away to someone in Brooklyn for this paint made the old-fashioned way—mortar and pestle, real ingredients—and he shows me the paint-maker's catalogue, one row after another typed on a Royal Deluxe typewriter. I recognize the typewriter because I have one on which I still type poems. I imagine Cliff with his guitar in a studio in Charleston, me at my typewriter five blocks away, and this man mixing his paint somewhere in Brooklyn, and I think of the space that opens between us—interior or exterior or a third thing. Again I think of being near but never at the space brothers share.

Tasks Before Pietà

One child in particular I have looked at again and again when I've visited Cliff's studio. It's a large painting of a child standing, a toddler really, but his feet square themselves and his hands are held out palm up as if he bears a weight. He carries something in his arms that has been painted out many times. He looks up slightly and seems to stand carrying all that is to be erased and has been erased (from the world, from him, even from parts of his body). Cliff says he has quit working on him but I see he keeps him hanging there, tacked to the studio wall. This is his process, to work with the canvas stretched only on tacks and flat to the studio wall until it is finished. To truly give the painting up he has to stop and take the painting down. He has to make the stretcher. I know Cliff to be an expert carpenter—he's told me he makes many stretchers at a time, cutting the wood and joining the corners deliberately, with a kind of patience. I can easily imagine him doing this—have almost asked to watch him do it. I think of O'Keeffe and her brother-helper, of the wood that snapped her largest stretched canvases, and the steel that held.

Because I grew up in church I find the boy to be a reverse pietà, but this is too specific an idea. He cannot, after all, carry his own body down from the cross any more than my older boy can shield the younger one from pain that is coming to him from a far distance, almost unseen on the horizon. Perhaps the distance from God to God is an erasure of self, the effacement of the known (self) on the cross of unknowing (others). Or it's the rusty leaking roof of the *morada*, adobe clay bleeding down as the men stand looking at each other before a single wound is opened. Among them the one who will be crucified. And the one who will hold the ropes. And the one who will hoist the cross. And the one who will take the man down. And the one who will rest his head on stone.

And the one who is not there. Who walks out into the hills the day before Easter and finds a cross, paints it black and thick with the brightest possible outline underneath of trapped sunset. And in these gestures of making, a distance opens where affliction is a grateful idea at once interior, exterior, and something else we only come near together.

Loose Thread • *four years after*

PAUL CELAN, ARSHILE GORKY

> I hear the axe has flowered,
> I hear the place can't be named,
> I hear the bread that looks on him
> heals the hanged man,
> the bread his wife baked him,
> I hear they call life
> the only refuge.
>
> —PAUL CELAN

When a loose thread needs pulling—though pulling it means, in some ways, untangling the present moment from *before*, in ways that admit the enormity of grief—that's when I write. What of the afterlife ties itself to the other end? What song will I hear whose voice might never again sing in my presence?

In the present moment, my two boys are arguing with children whom they love more than anything as friends visit on a lazy Saturday before Labor Day. But even so, there are too many children and too few adults, so after infractions only the children witnessed, our afternoon turns to a post-mortem of crimes that occurred when adult supervision lagged. The explanations dissemble into poorly understood grudges, willful misunderstandings. It's a drawn out and deeply felt disagreement in which one holds tight to his grain of truth, the thing that escalated the argument, and the other accuses him of *just making things up*.

Let the thread fall loose, I want to say. Love each other in short and fading light. All that knows you best, all that loves you back, is held within the walls of this room.

Instead, the thread that needs letting go pulls everything tight. After half an hour it could cut a diamond, and does: the shining day, one of the last that will be crisp and warm enough for outdoor play before winter comes—any game, pick it and go—yet all of them opt to stay inside. When a loose thread needs pulling, sometimes don't pull.

The way they argue over a narrative they all frame differently has me thinking about the ethics of the image, how a narrative sometimes detaches the image from its surroundings; in the case of argument, images can be produced to substitute for reason, to provide a tidy narrative, or to illustrate a wrong deeply felt, among many possibilities. The image's symbolism detaches it from the realities of the experience and from its original ethical framework.

Soon what was real once, shared between friends, becomes an instrument of individual interpretation, the image standing in for a set of ideas, ordering a world that might rightly remain pleasantly disordered forever had the arguer not brought an interpretation to bear. Severed from narrative, the image could have a different life; in our small dining room thick with discord, the image stays inside its narrative: someone is lying and someone is telling the truth. Or so the kids tell me. For now each takes their individual truth into a different privacy to cultivate it, and when the children go home, they will leave unsure when they'll again play as easily with each other as they once had.

Like the apostle Thomas presented with Christ's scars, I remain unsure about the assumptions attached to the process of moving *thing* toward *idea*. I wonder if the children, asking their pointed questions, wanted answers but didn't mean to hurt each other as they asked them. Maybe Thomas, asking as he did to see the scars on Christ's hands, did not need proof of Christ's suffering, but instead wanted to experience that suffering himself, to be with the scar as if he *was* the scar, the better to participate in the suffering of his friend. I don't tell the kids this, but seeing that each has a scar, I wish they could find a way to share rather than nurse them alone.

If friends could agree on "the real," what of "the real" might truce its way into a common understanding? For some aspects of the real, such an understanding can be found, but aren't others—I don't know what to say—too sacred for interrogation? These children who spend their Saturday arguing mightily over a soccer jersey have watched their playmates' parents pass them by disconsolate; some have attended the funerals of friends. The number lost was higher than some could count at the time, higher than the older ones want the younger ones to know.

Years have passed since the shooting at Sandy Hook School in our town—on this Saturday before the new school year starts, five Christmases stand between these children and that moment—and today, though their arguments seem trivial, their words have an edge. I don't pull that thread.

⁂

These days I live in fear of the catalog in poems, once a friend for its precision and the accretion of depth, even for its potential to surprise: I am fond of apples, tomatoes, and elocution exercises. But now, familiar with a catalog that lists names of children lost one after the other, I'm leery of the harm cataloging can do, grammar seeming to make inevitable their senseless murders, reducing their deaths into nothing more than a list.

Yet all is not thus. The beautiful world, in the shape of one ruby-necked hummingbird, intervenes and insists on being described. I hear her before I see: it's as if she has hovered in my inner ear, tiny motor of my ongoing survival. You've got it wrong, she says, jockeying just now for purchase on the feeder with two yellow jackets from an underground nest, the location of which keeps moving around the yard. She gets a spot on the feeder, they won't let her be there, she

flies away, she comes back determined. Her return is a re-
minder that work of all kinds goes on around us: being hun-
gry, needing to be fed. And Paul Celan hums in my ear, too,
reminding me life is *the only refuge*. Not knowing otherwise,
I don't get to say it's not. I don't get to decide about hunger.
Or ongoingness. Now the hummingbird takes a long drink
unimpeded, and the two retreating yellow jackets, having
called for reinforcements, seem upset from their vantage
alongside the woods where I imagine they are watching her.
This time they don't bother to return. Something has been
decided. They've let go of her thread.

The week has been long here; school has started. Like so
many others I have attached myself to school busses again.
Some days I have brought Luke late to the stop and had to
run up, him the last one on, and other days have come early
and stayed late enough to watch the bus finish its run and
U-turn back by our street. Those days my boy looks once
and wonders, surely, what in the world my day holds that I
can stand there so long. What am I so worried about that I
need to see him again?

I know that his return to school this year is different than
all the other years. In late July I told him the extent of the
tragedy; for five years, he's known only bits of it: that some
children in his circle of friends had lost friends he hadn't
met. This summer, the summer of the soccer-jersey fight,
going into fourth grade, he learned from me the relevant
pieces of information. That it *happened in a school, not yours,
but nearby—at Sandy Hook, the pretty school they just rebuilt.*
That he *didn't know any of the children because we were new*

to town when it happened. That he *can ask* me, his father, or his brother anything he needs to know, but *shouldn't ask at school.* I tell him this while driving him to a friend's travel baseball game, the summer league; he's a rectangle in my rearview surrounded by curvy summer roads. I ask if he has any questions, and he has one: *Why would you tell me here, now, while we are driving?* And he follows with a statement: *Such a big thing.* I say *because there's not a good time* and *I didn't want to make it a big deal.* I say this not because it isn't a big deal—of course it is—and not to diminish its importance. But because words are imperfect and I am imperfect, these are the words that come from me, his mother, on this occasion that may change his life forever. As much as I have done to prepare for this moment, the many days at my desk writing, the hours discussing the shooting with his father and his brother, words that would approach this event collapse into a common and inadequate phrase. Even so he seems to understand that what I wanted was to integrate this into what he knew of the world without taking that world entirely from him.

Several minutes pass as we ride together in silence, the *big thing* between us, around us, as it has been for years, but now newly shared. And with that I feel the thread loosen; temporarily, he seems to drop the *big thing* altogether. Or he doesn't drop it so much as choose not to say what he is thinking. Going forward from this moment, all quiets between us will hold inside them the possibility that he is thinking about it.

This year as he climbs on the bus, it's the first year I

know he knows the whole *story*, as if such a thing could be made into a *story*, fit with a story's penchant for interpretation, moral, and meaning, none of which I am able to supply. I am aware he thinks of it; it visits him and leaves as quickly as it came, a passing thought that is backdrop to many others as the bus pulls up and away towards the next stop. Or it stays and takes all the air on the bus. Or possibly both one after the other. I have no way of knowing.

We parents linger as the bus moves away. Where we can't see the children who don't get on the busses, we summon their images from pictures that circulated for weeks afterward; where we can't begin to imagine, an image substitutes. On these first school days as my son returns to the routine of the bus and to a new room on the top floor of the old part of the school he's been in since kindergarten—five years!—I have to acknowledge that for him, as for all of us, there remains a loose thread, something untied.

As school starts, as the busses reinstate their rounds, the not-here visits in ways I find wending into my work. The not-here is all around, even in pride of place at the back of the bus, where the fourth graders are *finally* the biggest kids. I remind myself that's not precisely true: the not-here would have been on the earlier bus, fifth grade, the one going to the intermediate school when it is still a little dark in the mornings. My boy was a year younger than they were then, and older now than each will ever be.

To write about what is not here, what has been forcibly taken—how could any vessel ever hold it, much less an imperfect one made of words? What's any image next to that? And what interpretation could ever begin to untangle our existence here from theirs, the dead from the living? Every new school year brings iconography as well as the absence of the real. What garment stitched from these tiny moments clothes those in the afterlife—too happy, or worried about us, or disappointed, to visit?

Is the thread that attaches me to my boy stronger or weaker bearing with it, as it does, this loss? No matter its tensile strength, it attaches me to him who barely looks back as he walks up the steps of the bus and on and to the back to his hard-earned spot (last seat!). Because he is merciful he answers my wave with a slight nod from the way-back window. His goalie gloves are on because he still thinks, though he is the smallest boy on the travel team, he will be picked as goalie at his first practice this week.

The thread is still there when, now travelling the other side of the road because the bus has made its U-turn at North Valley Field, my boy gives me an answering look (no wave now) as he sees I'm still at the stop. And the thread tightens but remains as the bus goes down Echo Valley, up Old Farm Hill, onto Schoolhouse Hill and then Evergreen, through three more neighborhoods until it reaches his school. Uncertainty remains, but I choose to believe the bus makes it to school—that interpretation allows me to keep the thread from cutting anything for the hours he is not with me.

All day, all through town, if I look I can almost see them: threads in the parking lots, in the supermarket aisles, at the

General Store where the public works men are already on their fifth hour of eight—threads that, though tight, don't snap, not today or not yet. Occasionally in one of these places I see someone whose thread is loose. These I would pick up if I could, but instead I offer a wave or a smile. At those moments I could not begin to describe what I see; nor should I, at least not with the clumsy imagery of the real: too much has escaped into contingency for me to trust the known world with what have become, through their loss, sacred threads.

✤

Not unlike the school friends arguing in my dining room, artists have argued their grudges in salons, sometimes with less at stake, sometimes with more (though more is hard to imagine). Not least of the arguers were the Surrealists, picking up any old thread and relishing its tight pull. The arguments were many: what was art and what wasn't, who was true and most devoted and most arch, what should be included under the broad banner of the "real." Since much of what they experienced *was* surreal, *having the quality of a dream*, they wanted their art to acknowledge that aspect of their perception; in fact, it was imperative to them that art acknowledge the surreal.

For the Surrealists, to make art without accounting for the violent disconnect between the real and what was *beyond* real ("sur") was to live in a fundamentally dishonest way. Their acceptance of the violent un-twinning of the present moment from its natural environment, their acknowledgment that an axe might flower, makes me grateful. This articulation mirrors my own dissatisfaction with the real. It helps me at the bus stop and the grocery store to know that others have questioned exactly how to represent the discord one feels between the quotidian and the extraordinarily untenable, both somehow housed in the now of one's experience.

Many of the Surrealists' arguments involved the issue of how closely an utterance could be related back to or drawn from life, and why divergence mattered. In the visual arts decades later, this argument would lead to clear battle lines drawn between painting a figure or choosing not to create an image based on or referring to recognizable figures, arguments that led to the *flowering axe* of Abstract Expressionism.

Among Surrealists there was a worry that the thread from image to image could be drawn too tight, that associations could grow so remote that the meaning connecting images could break down, so that too much work had to be done to connect an image to its meaning. Or worse, what if the image didn't connect to a meaning at all? Yet it's clear to me that images and meaning need not connect. In fact, meaning may be more truthful unmade than made. In a gift shop near my house I have watched a full basket of silver mantra bracelets dwindle over five years. All the ones that have sayings such as "choose love" or "you are home" are gone. Two identical ones remain, and both say *everything happens for a reason.*

There are moments when the meaning breaks, and what is necessary then is to acknowledge breakage. No false structure of meaning can be made to house the meaninglessness of some acts. Reason is not necessary—in fact is an intrusion—in these moments. The Surrealists addressed the issue of reason, interrogated it, and in some cases impeached it. When images don't help to order the world but instead highlight its inherent disorder, the artistic utterance can be used to make us newly aware that in fact the pieces of the puzzle of reality do *not* fit together, that underneath the thin fabric of a stitched together order, there is nothing but blue-black space. Such images are highly ethical works of art because they acknowledge that some threads must stay loose.

People in my town are not the first to experience this surreal existence grounded in a loss of reason, and though I wish it were true we aren't the last, either. Holocaust survivor Paul Celan inhabited that no-meaning place when he combined words into other words in order to come closer to showing how meaning broke down, using the language of his childhood German to catalog the precise ways meaning could leave a language. Using a natural tendency in German toward compound words, his work in French and then English took on a nearly impossibly high information load, thus realizing a tone that resisted interpretation, something the reader could not master intellectually but instead was forced entirely to feel: *Black milk of daybreak we drink it at evening / we drink it at midday and morning we drink it at night / we drink and we drink . . .*

We drink and we drink . . . . Back from morning bus drop-off to my feeder: the hummingbird is nervous at the low level of sugar water, so I hurry to mix more, mix more. As my fork circles, the sugar in the bowl disappears. It was there, a white swirl that danced on my fork in a one-to-four ratio of water and sugar, but now it has gone inside a solution. Never mind. The hummingbird has another problem: an adolescent pileated woodpecker likes the new brew and outranks her for now, bullying her off into some ordinary flowers, leftover from summer, and for now there are enough of those for her to survive. The black milk of daybreak is the work of looking for something to feed us, black work pacing itself with living need.

By the time my boy gets home the feeder is low again. I've not written anything more. He goes soundlessly inside his headphones to his video game. Maybe he'll be back when he's hungry.

Though the Surrealists' solution to appraising (even impeaching) meaning appeals to me, it's a flawed enterprise. Among its drawbacks, appraisal has the quality of not having been lived and must be interrupted (or narrated) in order to approximate lived experience. More importantly, appraisal's thread must hang loose in that it leaves unsolved the problem of what to do with the authority of the image. Won't the readers experience *any* image as an invitation to interpret, and therefore supply their meaning to it? Aren't the Surrealists, in their (childish) insistence on argument, simply drawing more tightly the snapping thread of theory?

Turns out they argued about this, too, and didn't agree. In 1913 Georges Duhamel accused Guillaume Apollinaire of "indulging in countless arbitrary and abortive images," warning that "the two terms of an image must always be connected by a secret thread," and that the thread should not be stretched so far it could snap. Yet Apollinaire knew the abortive image tells a certain kind of truth and refuses resolution in a way that can be its own testament, especially to those who have experienced sudden and irreversible trauma.

One painting I think of when I think of unmaking the image in response to trauma is *The Artist and His Mother* by Arshile Gorky, of which there are several versions; I have in front of me a reproduction of the one at the Whitney Museum of American Art. Gorky, a survivor of the Armenian Genocide, left many details unfinished or blurred in this famous painting, which he created by working from a photograph of his mother he kept with him all his life, though she died in his adolescence in the aftermath of their march to Russia from Armenia during the genocide. Gorky was the product of her second marriage; her first husband and eldest daughter had been killed in an earlier massacre, and she married a widower who had likewise lost his wife in that same event. In this sense, Gorky was a child of loose threads; to have made cogent "meaningful" connections would have sealed away whole parts of his (and his mother's) experience in a sort of non-existence, erasing them in favor of the unity of the picture plane. Instead, he flattened that plane until some images appeared as iconic death masks, others remained shadowed and textural, an act of calling attention to their representations in paint and interrupting the continuity of narrative. Many other portraits prove that Gorky was certainly capable of "working from life," of "finishing" an image from a photograph, yet every version of this painting he left unfinished—although there's a scholarly debate ongoing about whether these were images left unfinished, erased, or purposely blurred. What's clear is he left the seams showing, disallowing the image its life outside of the context of its having been made (and unmade).

Within the debate over the relationship of the image to meaning is where I like to think Gorky lived; because the image is one of a mother he lost in an event which precipitated not only his emigration to America but a re-invention of himself that included a new name—but not, it turned out, a loss of identity—Gorky decided the seams of un-meaning should show through. Because he could *hear* the axe flowering, he wanted everyone who saw his work to be able to hear it, too. Like Celan, he seems to be saying "I hear the place can't be named," even as he tries through an arch and precise visual language not to name but to fix that place in his memory. As you might imagine, his was a memory full of loose thread, requiring him to revise, erase, paint over, scrape through, and refuse cohesion in his work.

Gorky's blurred, erased, and eventually non-figurative style would inspire Willem de Kooning, Mark Rothko, Jackson Pollock, and others to hear how they couldn't name the place into which they were painting, and most credit

Gorky as the father (or at least older brother) of Abstract Expressionism. As Kim Servart Theriault notes about the Whitney version of *The Artist and His Mother* in the retrospective catalog of the 2010 exhibition at the Philadelphia Museum of Art, there is "an inherent tension between the figures that is created by the negative space between them. The figures do not touch but are kept apart by a narrow band in the very top layer of paint, most likely added in the painting's final stages." Rather than erased or unfinished, the barrier between mother and son is imposed as a final gesture, a gesture that covers a deeper thread, but also separates them. Perhaps this under-layer "unfinishes" the image; buried underneath, it unsettles and unrooms the easy stitch of narrative.

Even here, early in Gorky's work, and thereafter for the many years he continued to keep this version of the painting in his studio, he took as his subject the interrogation of the image. Later paintings continue to explore, as he did with this narrow band of paint between the subjects, the relationship of one image to the next. Even as he honored the "real," the "record" of his past as captured by the photograph, he added the painterly equivalent to Celan's doubt, acknowledging through the blurring of the image that all reality and any representation of it could only ever be hearsay: "I hear they call life / the only refuge." The hearsay quality created the blur as well as the floating context (or un-context) for the image.

But an image, no matter how divorced from its "mother," invites from the viewer a tendency to try to relate back to another "story," whether in paint or in language. To disrupt the seamlessness of the narrative impulse, the artist represents not only the image but also the struggle the image has seen in its making. Yet a mother is never *unrelated* to a son, of course. Theriault notes that in another version of the painting "the boy's lap is the same color as the mother's upper arm. The light color of her dress seems almost to have washed over his left foot, acting like a scrim." Here the tonal color of the painting connects the two, even as genocide begins to tighten the thread that connects them, until it snaps; the snapped thread is what Gorky has remade inside—underneath—the portrait.

Theriault posits that Gorky wrestled with whether and what to represent in art of one's suffering: "reliving or depicting trauma can be problematic because it perpetuates victimhood." This dilemma is similar to the Surrealists' ethical dilemma: how realistically should one portray experience as uninterrupted, as interpretable? It's also the problem of the bus stop for me. Gorky's answer is something Theriault calls "reconfiguration," writing that "Gorky's work is a figurative reassembling of time, space, and place. His 'in-betweenness' informed his style." She concludes that the way Gorky reconciles irreconcilable loss in his work is to disassociate it from its original context: he reassembles it figuratively, in ways that make the connection between object and image more tenuous—make it, even, to use the Surrealists' word, "abortive." Like Apollinaire, Gorky could be accused of not allowing "the two terms of an image" to "be connected by a secret thread," but instead choosing to reveal that the thread is not adequate to the stitching together of meaning. This technique—creating abstract work to call into question the resolution of experience by the safety of theoretical frameworks—becomes a tenet of modern art, so commonplace now that we have a political saying to describe it: a sane reaction to an insane situation.

I like to think that Gorky leaves the seams showing because broken parts shine truest; I know my own unruly images no longer find their places inside punctuation, much less a narrative, when I am writing a poem. Gorky's mother's hands are fleshy clubs that blend in hue with her apron—connections can be drawn, but not depended upon. Shapes can represent what they are, but can never totally cohere. Celan can talk of milk so long has he tells us it is *black*; doing so gives the familiar its sacred and proper tinge of dissonance (and death).

‎‎‎⁊

With fellow surrealist André Breton's help, Gorky sat and named many of his paintings in a few afternoons during which he simply talked about his childhood while Breton took notes, though again and again Gorky insisted the paintings were not full of figures but rather of shapes in space. On one such occasion Breton, listening hard to Gorky, named one late work *How My Mother's Embroidered Apron Unfolds in*

My Life: it is a dripping painting full of what might be called abortive images—Gorky called them "biomorphs"—which connected to figuration through the image of the apron that appeared in the title. The painting itself he would never quite let finish, never fully organize around a closed and resolvable narrative.

And so it is within the cosmology of grief that what remains may be properly represented only as unfinished work. How could such work be otherwise and remain remotely true? Gorky himself felt his paintings were catalogs of suffering, so much so that he once responded to a MOMA questionnaire about whether a drawing had "any personal, topical, or symbolic significance" by saying simply "wounded birds, poverty, and one whole week of rain." As I find that quotation in the catalog, Luke comes to tell me he is *tired, cold,* and has *a scratchy throat.* He has not come to me when he is hungry (like the hummingbird) but when he is sick. How like Gorky he sounds!

My son crawls into my lap and folds himself so he fits, something that he will not do much longer, as he is all knees and elbows, poised to grow. I have stopped my writing for now. It occurs to me that my answer about the relationship of the image to living grief is not to be found on the page. Intimate if not simultaneous, image and grief instantiate each other in the momentary. As probably as not, my boy on my lap is an abortive image. Even so, there is no school bus to take him anywhere soon; for the moment the thread between my boy and me is marvelously—terrifyingly—loose.

A Covering Snow • *three years after*

HÉLÈNE CIXOUS, PABLO PICASSO,
GUILLAUME APOLLINAIRE

Captivity

Again we've dragged the boys to midtown Manhattan, the
both of them inclined instead toward the park or street food,
toward anything else, but we go to *Picasso Sculpture* at the
MOMA, explaining that rather than the flat paintings they
critique as *not as good as what we do* they'll be seeing sculp-
ture, ideas made plastic. Some of the pieces, I've heard or
read somewhere, are just folded paper napkins Picasso made
to please a bored sister at a restaurant, the kind of thing the
boys do when they're feeling generous toward each other.
The story partly entices and partly annoys them. We're in-
side an ongoing debate about the efficacy of Modern Art in
general; their interest in gathering material means they will
be quiet through the rooms, assembling arguments for the
drive home. How wrong we are to want to travel all this
way to look at these pieces, they'll say, having looked none-
theless, moving steadily one room ahead of me so that I am

quickly alone, intermittently so; it's them as much as Picasso creating that space around me, causing me for a moment to be aware of some limitation I can't name.

Bird, Plaster, 1931–32

In the fifth room I see it: *Bird*. It's white and sits on its belly (no feet), perhaps a foot long and half a foot wide, as the artist began early on to try everything at his disposal to grow, change, see, and feel the contours of both the inner and the outer landscape. So: bike seats, heating elements, paper, sand, springs, sheet metal, colanders. For *Bird*: humble plaster for a simple upturned head and flayed wings. Later in the car I will try but fail to explain that when I look at this small shape surrounded by larger bodies I think *worship*. I think *praise*.

Has a little bit of the human capacity to gaze in wonder at the body of a foreign thing (and at the foreign in us) entered the artist's hand and transmitted into this bird? I can feel it suffusing the plaster as hundreds swirl past, catching the exhibition in its closing days. Hélène Cixous—discussing Derrida, searching, really, for him—describes (with some difficulty) the effort to know the inside self, in this case through the act of reading a book: *At the beginning of this whole book, to begin, there will have been this moment of separation within me, the instant of opening what must remain closed, and then, the dazzling effusion of blood, frightening, sudden appearance of what can only be interior.*

What is this moment of separation? Surely I've felt it, here at the museum, or when I am away from someone I love, or when I am away from myself, untrue to an interior *effusion*. The famous book she is discussing is Derrida's *Circonfession* (in English, *Circumfession*). I am not a good student and have not read it—but to my blood-born poet's ear the word's a mix of confession and circumference, both the long way around. It's a *making* and a *try*.

Something of the moment of separation visits me in front of this bird the longer I stand with it, though *with* is an inadequacy of language to capture what I do as I stay near this bird. Perched head up, tail up, the bird asks what is *interior*, what is *exterior*, what is *not me*? *Nothing is not me*, I would tell bird through glass. *You are me, you are the one I choose*—not those in the other galleries, eleven in all, spanning sixty-two years of work. Bent absinthe spoons, burned cardboard guitars, the lion design that would end up fifty feet high in a park in Chicago. Them too, them later. But first *you*: your attenuated plaster mirrors me. Look at how foreign my hands become standing in front of you, trying to take your picture. My hands are no more mine than yours.

Finally I leave him in his glass box. My blood is back under the membrane of my skin and I sense it coursing. I go from circa 1930–32 through several more rooms. I am working my way up to The War Years.

Breath Work

Night terrors, or their possibility, mean my younger boy is asleep in our bed. The night after the Picasso exhibition, awake but not moving much among sleepers, a song's in my head, perhaps related to the bird, perhaps not. Like a bird's wing its phrasing would fold into the prose of Cixous, but though the words are mine not hers I don't know what they mean or why Cixous has anything to say about Picasso or me or the plaster bird: *My wound is the door. My insomnia is the wound.*

It's not insomnia that I have exactly. It's not a problem the way a wound is not, actually, a problem. It's a problem the way anything noticed or felt enough to wound is a *dazzling effusion.* At the moment of waking—dazzling, effusive—I am outside my body. And the outside is full of the artifacts of inside; perhaps this is part of what drew Picasso to his materials, since using them pushed him inside himself, the better to show on the outside the possibilities he'd been harboring in interior travels and in dreams.

My insomnia acts as a pleasing wound. One minute asleep, the next pleasantly awake. My boy is next to me on one side, my husband on the other, and I have the room to turn my head and look out beyond the rise/fall of his small sculptural form to the tree that is my all-weather companion. I am pleasantly awake outside my body, and also asleep in the tree's swaying wind. How cold is it? What time is it where I am (where am I)?

Where I am, the engine of my boy being alive is not far from me, or not yet far from me. Even so, sometimes there is glass between my bird and me. And outside my body I am not necessarily anything but a wound in wind.

On Doors

Cixous, on the concept of the door, that keeper of inside / outside, remarks: *first vision, which acted then, for me, without my knowledge, like the revelation of a door. There is a door. In the world, there are doors.*

...*first vision, which acted then*: it's possible in speaking of first vision Cixous is talking about a childhood consciousness, revelation acting upon her without her conscious knowledge. She is not the first to link the artistic impulse to childhood habits of mind, but probably everyone (not only the artistic genius) has felt this. My boys identify this as the essential fraud of Modern Art, that the resulting art is child's play, although in making their very argument I fear they strip themselves from *first vision* in favor of the posture of critique.

Their argument is not entirely wrong or new. Picasso himself would agree, having famously said, "Every child is an artist. The problem is how to remain an artist once we grow up." Some may not remember first vision or consciously perceive it until asked to do so by the object of art—painting, sculpture, poem. Children, frequently visited by (and so closer to) spiritual experience, seem to drop down the well of spirit more readily than adults; adulthood can be seen as a mopping up of what washed out of us (blood and other things) while we were children.

❧

The argument that reconciles the boys' point of view and mine is that part of the artist's job is to recall that state children easily enter as if passing through a doorway where the door has been removed, as if passing through air. But describing it that way simplifies matters, since a piece of the artist's task is the elimination of the idea of the door. So, not simply to step through the open doorway, the doorless door, but to conceptualize the opening as never having been framed by the door: this is the state of childhood and the task of the artist.

Part of this artistic, childhood temperament is a fidelity to a close proximity with the outside world. In my case that was a world of wind, sand, and ocean. From a vastness, creatures were spit up out of deep places during many-headed and frequent storms. The reckoning with these sometimes pleasing, sometimes frightening other beings led to intermittent but violent confrontations with people and events around me. How does one reconcile the shock of what is truly new and wild with the awareness that that thing is here, in the world, along with team sports and television? In my case I spent my days in tidal pools awaiting my father's homecoming from his work designing rockets, waiting for the moment his Skilcraft pen with its brushed silver band tucked neatly into his front pocket was mine for the evening, strange as any creature I'd found that day. All evening in front of the news I'd worry the band loose between forefinger and thumb. What had the pen's band to do with the pools of unnamed creatures? I accepted their reticulation; I lived inside their strangeness.

The adult who has foregone *first vision* approaches material with a curiosity, the artist with a recovered or restored wonder. The materials Picasso finds wash ashore everywhere in the sculptural, plastic world. Wire, body, body, cardboard. Torn and scratched paper. Bird. Each is a trove found on the beach, collected for no other reason but wonder.

Grown

I was already grown when I pressed too hard on a wall and a small door opened. By this time I had lost the sense of connection between myself and things; I had not worried a band off its pen or seen something move in a moving tide in a long time. But in that moment—I could hear the metal mechanism click, could feel the hinged panel spring towards me—the wonder, the fear, and the desire to feel that had driven me into the state of child suddenly awakened. On the other side of the not-door was a chamber, a shelf with a mason jar on which a piece of masking tape had been placed, on which had been written *orchid food*. And so it was that I learned the wonder of the foreign, and its innateness in me, could be a function of language. Any time two words are put together for what might be the first time a door inside language snaps open.

About the door, Cixous continues:

> Happily there isn't only the world. Beyond the world is the Other side. One can pass over, it's open or it opens. Happily one can go there. Where? There.
> (How?) We need a door.

As regards artistic exploration, the question of whether the door is already open or whether it opens with added pressure is an important one. If one is bent on true exploration, there are many kinds of pressure points: Picasso's material, poetic language, our own foreignness, the curiosity of the love of another. Each supplies a certain amount of pressure to open the door, but how much pressure to apply? What is the difference between noting the door's opening and blowing through the wall oneself (without bothering to look for a door)? A dazzling effusion of the self into the world, Picasso's figures implore from the gallery: *apply all pressure! Open us wider!*

There's the door of wind in the tree. The door of my boy's breath and what it does to me to acknowledge it, to match it, track it with my own. There is the open question of what parts stay inside of him, parts I don't and will never touch. And parts I can't get *out of me* to give him, to give to the outer world. The outer world, I know, includes him.

On the Relationship of Art to the Body

The bird sings white. From its glass it adopts a pose of worship. It sings plaster. It calls for someone's hands to press hard, to get *out* what had been *in*.

For Cixous, out-and-in is both an essential and an unbearable separation. That resonates both with my experience of the bird and the sleeping body of my son. Intrinsic to the edge of fear that creeps into me as I listen for his breathing is the question of death, what Cixous calls *the only absolutely 'impassable' border*. But also love: *The uprooted heart in the heart, in the outside interior of me. There is an outside of me.*

There is an outside of me. These six words describe the paradox of love. In the moment of knowing that one's own happiness is tied to another, that one's own well-being is no longer the most important thing, a door should open to an inside. Instead, one realizes that there is an outside of me, something I can't protect. Something likely to suffer or even die. This is the terrifying and somewhat unthinkable truth: we are not outside ourselves but rather stuck inside, watching parts that are outside-of-us walk around, jump too high, cross the street without looking, enter their classroom.

Outside is a bear in the woods, a stalking beast; but that bear is also in me. I'm the wild animal. A bear's been seen at my boys' bus stop minutes after they were there. Upturning the trash cans, searching for food. *Me me me.*

But this pressure between the outside that is me and the inside that is me is also the thing pressing down, drawing me to the desk, putting Picasso hands deep in the clay (the clay is me, the bird is me, and the pressure is me).

On Material Submission

Faith traditions—like artistic practices, in the sense that they too abjure the body—insist on submission of the real in order to access the unseen as a necessary condition of creation.

In every room of *Picasso Sculpture*, I get the sense of the artist submitting himself to the materials at hand. Each room is a new place with newly discovered limitations, and those limitations are simultaneously internal and external. One limitation is material (as blood limits body). *Happily there isn't only the world*, Cixous says, but as in any practice that is place-bound (and all practices are place-bound, as well as bound by material), Picasso uses limitation as medium. The medium is something to lean against, restraint become rigor and creative force. Inside his body, yes, every abstract idea, every roiling philosophy, great breakers of supposition and fear, but outside of his body, the materials at hand offer a stay against total abstraction, and provide a resting place from interior fallacy. Outside-in-me is concrete—full of wind, plaster, boys, and birds.

Hence the integrity of Picasso's small wall-mounted pieces, among them a canvas turned backwards to make a shallow box: *Object with Palm Leaf.* The description below the title is *cardboard, plants, nails, and objects sewn and glued to back of canvas and stretcher and coated with sand. Sand partially painted.*

Sand partially painted as a piece of language becomes birdsong, prayer, and rainfall. Outside becomes interior if a tender attention is shown. Painting sand, the uselessness and idleness of the act, creates an interior pressure on the piece that speaks to the urgency of the enterprise. Let's make something with nothing, it says. And in doing so something in me will go outside, something outside will come in.

Object with Palm Leaf is a small box; there are larger pieces, public in nature, which share the gallery, but nearby, the companion to *Palm Leaf* is called *Composition with Glove.* (*Glove, cardboard, and plants sewn and glued to back of canvas and stretcher and coated with sand. Sand partially painted.*) Both were completed contemporaneously with the wire sculptures Picasso submitted to a committee deciding on a memorial for the poet Guillaume Apollinaire. In time the committee rejected all of them. Perhaps tired of repeated tries or aware of the fallacy of monument—How with wire, brass, or bronze to honor such a man as Apollinaire?— Picasso took refuge in Juan-les-Pins, a seaside town in the Cote d'Azur. There he found his new limitation: palms and sand. We can assume Apollinaire would approve Picasso's small monument, his limitation.

About a poem by Apollinaire, Edward Hirsch writes, "the poem appeals to the eye. It has a shapely dimension and thus relates to the plastic arts, especially painting." As an example of the concrete in poetry, he cites Apollinaire's "*Il pleut*" ("It's Raining"), which is typed so that the lines resemble "rain running downward across a windowpane."

The melancholy subject—routine inside the "material" of rain—soon opens its universe of possibilities; as the rain falls, Apollinaire suggests we "listen to the bonds fall off which hold you above and below." Before the poet mentioned this we had not known we were enslaved, but of course now we see our mistake. Captivity, one of Cixous's pet concepts, is sometimes (even often) invisible. By increments are we led to see that our bondage is both internal and external ("above and below").

On Bondage

That we are trapped in our bodies and in our own subjectivity is taken up at length by many modern writers and artists, among my favorites the poet James Wright: in "A Blessing," while touching a horse's ear, he tells us "suddenly I realize / that if I stepped out of my body I would break / into blossom." And Cixous talks about the problem of being in the body, a problem relieved by the momentary freedom of loving another:

> A foreignness separates the two from all humanity.
> Something that beats in their flesh, a blood perhaps,
> acts like a silent shibboleth. Neither seen nor known
> the two pass into their secret country. The door to the
> country is the first look. We enter one through the
> other. We are there. It's like having entered into the
> answer itself. The one that was waiting for us. And

immediately the foreign seizes us, already it flows, all strange, in our veins.

This union, interestingly a first look (like that which children experience) leads to new problems, problems that visit me in my predawn hours with my son. Wright's formulation of the limitation is "They love each other. / There is no loneliness like theirs." The foreignness of another restores in us the foreign in ourselves, avails us of the great universe of unknowns that we carry in our blood, our bodies a "secret country." It's not that we must empathize with the other; it is that we are the other. Creating art or writing poetry: each attempt at expression is an externalization of the essential problem of the foreign in us.

In that context, self-love is both obstacle and unattainable gift.

Apollinaire again, aware a raincloud is as good a lover as any: "those rearing clouds begin to neigh a whole universe of auricular cities." Once the bonds fall off inside our "first look" at another and we begin to understand our own vastness, our wildness neighs at us. Love of the parent for a child, or a face's love of rain, or the love of two horses—each becomes the other. Love is circumference.

On Free Love

Speaking of love: love of the title, the impulse to name. Through eleven galleries, sixty-two years spent wrestling with limitation (the material, the place, the limits of self-knowledge and self-love), working the better to see, hear, feel the strange in his own veins—Picasso sometimes puns. Among the revelations brought on by news of one's own foreignness: one thing resembles all things.

My favorite of Picasso's puns—in a pair of sculptures both named *Eye* and wall-mounted to the left of *Bird*—is that you have to look at the title to see that an eye is what each is, because otherwise each is a woman's labia with a baby crowning. The material (unlimited, or limited by what remains unnamed) is *plaster with iron-wire hook*.

This was Gallery 5, post-Apollinaire-Monument-Failure and pre-The-War-Years.

While I have been reworking this section, after the boys have climbed the steps of their busses (without bears), leaving the house with just me to fill it, my water has boiled away in its pot on the stove and left white mineral deposits meant for my bloodstream. But I needed to stay put and see where this part was leading before I could get back inside my body, though I heard the water going up into the air, a reverse of Apollinairean rain.

And Speaking of Bondage

I have left this part of the essay to sleep and have awoken with another strange Cixous-transliteration, my words from her "world." In my dreams Picasso's *Bird* mates or talks with another sculpture called *Death's Head*. I can't find the door of approach to this subject yet. Instead, my own words on a scrap of paper: *You are tired of holes bubbling up through wounds, of ponds eyed with white.* The work of knowing the foreign in me leads, incrementally, to my loving more of the world, more of the outside. I know this, but where do I end and where does the world begin?

Cixous's answer, one of many: *I am the finite that wants the infinite. Love infinites me. Without you I am a pebble, and my skin closes narrowly over me.*

Without you I am a pebble. Over this language my skin closes narrowly. Or rents itself open. A Picasso gallery note provides the information that five wooden figures (four called *Standing Woman,* one called *Seated Woman,* each narrow, eighteen inches "tall," all in a case together) are made of fir, some taken from "the backs of stretchers," some foraged from "the forest floor." This is perhaps my favorite gloss on any exhibition wall. I much prefer no gloss at all but year, place, and list of materials. Here, the list of materials itself opens a *door:* some are the backs of stretchers, some have been foraged from the forest floor. The tenderness of it, a lineage of woods wild and tame, kept apart till the artist applies his particular attention (a pressure). I think of the bones in my body, my boys' bodies, together in their places, not yet foraged, not yet tame.

Cixous, pertaining to what can be achieved in a life dedicated to circumferential confession, to searching for the love that is product and sum of searching, writes: *Then, under the shock of incredulity, one tries out circonfession: attempt to make oneself spit out the most secret blood so as to try to see with one's own eyes the interior color—of what?—of one's own spirit, the personal juice of life, inner proof of the existence of self.*

Picasso's *spit out secret blood*, his interior color, was fir foraged from the forest floor. Sand partially painted. *Inner proof of the existence of self.* And that proof restores a curiosity. If the self exists, let me find for it its open spaces.

Antlers

Eventually we are no longer trapped, we are momentarily free. This is both comforting and terrifying.

At the afternoon bus stop where no one has been mauled by a bear, as I wait for my younger boy (the one whose breath accompanies my insomnia), a high school boy comes walking up from the far end of a cul-de-sac. The high school kids get out early and he is in charge of his dogs, so he has given them a good long walk after they've waited for him all day. Behind the cul-de-sac are a pump station and a path that runs into a wild woods, past a vineyard to near the river. He has been walking his blue-tick hound and Irish setter. For a moment all three are wild, something of their *most secret blood* still visible.

I am the first human they have seen; I am part of their reluctant return, and also part of their foreignness. The boy pauses, in his hand one half of a rack of antlers from what was once a ten-point buck. We marvel at it together in a big silence; it is extraordinary. We try to imagine the breadth of this span when attached to a living beast. He points out a chip on a lower point where something smaller has tried to move the body of the buck, heavy and newly dead. Time collapses. Living and dead change places. I'm wild now, or we are. We're the mystery. *Love infinites us.*

I don't tell the high school boy about Picasso's famous bike-seat bull with handlebar horns (*Bull's Head*), mounted in triumph at MOMA but hidden in a bathroom in Paris all through The War Years. This was the piece that won me the argument about art with the boys; the piece they couldn't have done. I don't tell this half-wild dog-walker about *The Death's Head* rising up in bronze from a nearby white display table and resembling a burn victim, its face frozen and its nose collapsed, secreted by Picasso to the foundry to be fired in the dead of night lest the occupying Nazis find him practicing his art, the ultimate interior act made exterior, one that could have cost him his life. I don't approach The War Years with the boy because I am not totally free. And I can see he may yet be.

He tells me that tomorrow he will go back and look for the antler's other half, try to restore to the beast his crown, because if he doesn't, the day after that a covering snow is coming to bury it.

No Sheltered World · *after five years*

Agnes Martin, Tomas Tranströmer

Not Quite Square

By six months I have missed Agnes Martin's retrospective
show at the Guggenheim that closed in January, and so all
through June I am spending time with her in the museum
catalog and with interviews spliced into videos I find online
of the artist herself in front of half-made paintings. The ex-
hibition originated at the Tate Modern in London, travelled
to the Kunstsammlung Nordrhein-Westfalen in Düsseldorf,
the Los Angeles County Museum of Art, and finally to the
Guggenheim in New York. A catalog's no substitute, espe-
cially for Martin's large-scale paintings which employ the
palest color washes, but I have twice stood in front of her
grids, one at the small but lovely Aldrich Museum in leafy
Ridgefield, Connecticut, the other at the MOMA in New
York in a show clustering together women of the Abstract
movement, so I know the deeply emotional experience of
approaching her work from a distance and realizing as one
comes closer what once looked ready-made was made by

105

hand, composed of a series of almost incomprehensibly numerous marks of pencil and paint.

Deliberately not quite square, she liked to say of her paintings, noting that the rectangle (of which there were many in her work) upset the square, even *destroyed* it. And it's true: Martin's work is a battle of epic proportions played out in near tranquility. *Let the order go*, the paintings seem to say. Come close, be dedicated, but then in the service of your own quilted emotions, their narrow threads and ribbons, *let the order go*.

Over the years the answers Martin gave to her many questioners and admirers have taken on the quality of mantra. Spliced against Martin standing still in front of a canvas, or sitting in the chair in which she waited (sometimes for twenty years, she said) for inspiration, or overheard in the sound of her being interviewed atop video of her making her precise marks, some veer toward manifesto, others to documentary. One oft-cited one: *The goal is happiness*.

Of the grid when she first came to employ it she said she thought of *the innocence of trees*. Another video shows an elderly Martin stepping away from a line of paint, brush still wet, exhaling, saying *that one gave me some trouble*. And a little later in the same film, *I've got to sit down for a minute*.

But more often than not the trouble or effort of art making is not emphasized by Martin; instead she dwells in transformative possibility. As it was in the paintings, seemingly effortless at a middle distance, so it is with the artist: Martin emphasizes the lightness with which the work was approached. Art with the goal of *happiness* would be approached in this manner.

After thinking of *the innocence of trees* that provided her with the grid idea, Martin says, *And so I painted it and then I was satisfied.* Inside that last statement is buried a distinction between happiness and satisfaction, the difference, perhaps, between the unreachable and the temporary but possible. In art, snail-trail trace of journey is hand-made, striated with itself, its pocks and ridges (like a canvas) showing themselves to be more and more impactful the longer one remains devoted, as looker or maker. Or so it is in front of a Martin canvas.

In front of *The Tree* (1964) in the MOMA, my son Willem asks me how she made the lines so straight. We are drawn into the canvas by irregularity, as into seawater soon awash in small imperfections the way we might be if we looked down at our hands underwater newly strange seen distorted by sea particles and sand. I'd read that Martin tacked a string from one side of the canvas to the other, then followed it with her pencil. And there's a picture in her studio from 1960 of Martin, in quilted jacket and pants, in front of a primed canvas, her hair pulled back in a braid, moving a small ladder with the flat of one hand while the other holds a level that is nearly the width of the painting. In the next moment I imagine she climbs up, places the level so the bubble finds its place between two lines, and traces with graphite the mark that will join all the other marks until they come to sing.

Coming home from the museum, on the radio there is a story about a flooded river in Texas, which includes a warning that red ants can skim along the surface in great colonies resembling long red ribbons. Without our saying so, these connect somehow to Martin's lines—what they do in concert, great colonies of ribbons.

The Problem of Happiness

According to Martin there is no problem, really, with happiness. The problem is more to do with time. All the things one does inside it that can be devotion made into incremental measurements. "All I think about is painting," Martin told one interviewer. In yoga they say to mark time like this: *I am breathing in, I am breathing out.*

In the realm of the abstract the title is a worldly thing, a tether back to viewer, and a tether to time. Sometimes Martin's titles refer to time explicitly, or simply by the date, which can accompany the title of *Untitled*, but often time appears in the title as well. Other titles seem to refer to states of being, moments with others or with nature, such as *Falling Blue*, *White Flower*, *Song*, *Buds*, and *Little Sister*, all attributed to the early 1960s.

To my younger boy Luke, a draftsman himself, I bring the museum catalog open to *Summer, 1964*. At first I think this particular canvas has not been stretched as tightly, so the grid undulates, and the color is a deep summer blue, the kind you find in cotton towels washed many times and left on a line to dry. Then reading the notes I see it's not canvas at all but paper, and smaller than the large paintings, not wall-size but square and small, two feet by two feet. Even photographed in the catalog the paper moves. Inside each square, and there are 35 down the side by 47 across the top (1,645 in all), has been placed a small white dot of paint. As I move my finger to count the small squares, I see many that are, as Agnes said, actually rectangles: *My formats are square, but the grids never are absolutely square; they are rectangles, a little bit off square, making a sort of contradiction.*

I say to Luke, *When you are in front of this you can't not feel something, right?* He says, *No—nothing.* I want to convince him to see or feel, to respond, but he's playing a game of not responding. I persist, say she hand made each line, that each canvas required pages of numbers, all this math (another fondness of his), to figure out how many rows to make. I mention that math and art aren't unrelated, which he's figured out already from composing music, a piece called *Sweet Night* tethered, as is *Summer, 1964*, to time. I turn to the page in the catalog with the studio picture, show him her hair in the braid, the level and ladder, all the work of it, all that devotion. He himself is a very devoted draftsman, working in silence through one eraser, then the next, getting up only to sharpen his pencil or find another sheet of paper, the right one.

No, no, no, he answers calmly to each question I pose.

When I cover the square with rectangles, it lightens the weight of the square, destroys its power. Agnes again, finishing her thought on the rectangle. I can't help thinking *No* makes a kind of square shape, but Luke has left the open book. I hear the mouse clicking from inside the house as he defeats some digital foe.

And I am surprised to find I'm not unhappy with this exchange. How can I be, while the folds of *Summer, 1964* undulate from flat paper?

Three Times at the Wheat Harvest

As for most artists, the pressure to create (internal, intrinsic) and the pressure to support oneself (extrinsic) found themselves at odds, and for Martin there were periods when work was not possible due to her schizophrenia. There were happy times in New York with fellow artists with whom her ideas could mix (especially influential seems to have been the warp and weft of the textile artists, which helped Agnes not only with coming to the grid but with the sense of the hand-made inside the manufactured), and then a long period when she didn't paint (five years, from the time she left New York with a camper van to travel west until she fully settled in New Mexico), followed by a very productive few decades in which she developed much of the work for which she is now known.

In a journal, Agnes listed all her part-time jobs. Arne Glimcher, founder of the Pace Gallery and Martin's dealer for many years, included the handwritten note in a collection of her works and writings that he published after her death.

on a farm—milking . . . three times at the wheat
harvest . . . managed cherry pickers . . . taught three
years in country schools . . . packing ice cream . . . as
a disciplinarian worked with deprived boys . . . also
raised rabbits and ducks.

At the top of the list of jobs, Martin has written *Please publish all or none.*

In New Mexico with help from an assistant, she made an adobe house and lived there alone without common conveniences (water, electricity) for a few years. Then they built a studio and there she began to work again, first screen-printing, on the occasion of an invitation for an exhibition. This was 1973. She called the first series *On a Clear Day.* After that she was back, and she would work inside various series of paintings for the rest of her life.

It's not clear the period in her life the list of part-time jobs recounts, or if the list retrospectively accounted for a lifetime. *Painter* does not appear on the list, a sign that this was avocation rather than work.

In Situ Looking

Years ago in Florence before we had children, my husband and I visited the Museo de San Marco, a Dominican monastery-turned-museum, where the Renaissance painter Fra Angelico—himself a brother of the order—had painted a fresco on the wall of each of his brothers' rooms, the better for them to meditate and find themselves closer to God. His is art made for worship and reflection, such reflection as befits monk's vocation and avocation. He painted the very grand *Annunciation* for them, too, at pride of place on the landing at the top of the stairs before you turn to enter the dormitory hallway, but visitors are drawn to the repetition of these frescoes, each a different rendering of the crucifixion or pietà. The differences are small but important. The longer you look, the vaster they get.

Dean Young, in *The Art of Recklessness*, writes:

> "Say you think life is trembling," wrote Willem de Kooning of an idea he picked up in Kierkegaard. "Pretty soon everything trembles. Raphael trembles. Poussin trembles." De Kooning's point is that it doesn't matter so much what you think as you think it with a conviction that arises from the closely observed and considered world itself.

At the Museo de San Marco, my husband, still young, approached me with a discovery: If you place yourself at the very center of the dormitory hallway, get on your knees, and "walk" on your knees down the center hall, stopping at every room, then the arch of the doorway matches precisely the arch the artist painted within each fresco. Art rewards a viewer's devotion. We left that day with bruises on our knees and a blurry relationship to the world, so close were we to its trembling. I found out a week later I was pregnant with our first child, Willem.

I can only imagine Martin's large square paintings on

the ramps at the Guggenheim; I imagine myself walking on my knees there, as I did at the Museo. I wonder whether, as at the MOMA, curators wisely placed benches for sitting so that Martin's work could do its work of commanding devotion on the viewer over time. There is a value in viewing the very close, the middle, and the far distance in Martin's work, and in the Guggenheim all of those would be available.

When I lament to my husband, for instance, the difference between seeing Rauschenberg's work at the Guggenheim in 1994 and again at the MOMA this year, he says yes, architecture makes a work more grand. I remember him on his knees at the Museo, but he's thinking of Rauschenberg's *Hoarfrost* backlit and moving in currents of air on the Guggenheim ramps, as opposed to as we've just seen it in the MOMA: still lovely, a scrim of bedclothes, full of possibility but now tacked to a wall, its motion constrained.

With Martin at the Guggenheim, I can imagine how the viewer would stand and look at the pale bands of color from across the rotunda, then approach to see the painting at nose distance, almost exactly where the woman herself had stood with her level, making first one mark then the next, acts of deliberate and repeated devotion not unlike Angelico's repetitions for his brothers. Pretty soon everything trembles.

The Hand that Holds the Level

The hand that holds the level trembles, too. Therein lies the emotion to be gathered and harvested within Martin's work, its "shimmering" quality, to use another word favored by critics. About *On a Clear Day, 1973*, Martin wrote in a note to the viewer:

> These prints express innocense [sic] of mind. If you
> can go with them and hold your mind as emty [sic]
> and tranquil as they are and recognize your feelings at
> the same time you will realize your full response
> to this work.

Counting forward from the day at the Museo, it would be a decade and a half before I stood with Willem at MOMA and explained about Agnes, the level, and the bubble, both of us a nose away from her imperfect lines in *The Tree*, the very painting she cites as originating the concept of the grid. By that time he has already been to Florence and done the devoted knee-walk his father discovered while he was in utero. Perhaps because this type of practice is inhered in him, he is excited to read about her remark on *the innocence of trees* and takes a picture of the gallery-gloss language to think about later.

The innocence of trees, sure, that's apprehensible. But what can I tell Willem of the difficulty of the task that Martin describes above—to hold your mind *as empty and tranquil as [the paintings] are* and further, to *recognize your feelings at the same time*. Both tasks are difficult, but together, they seem impossible, since Martin's work comes to its emptiness through a journey that includes great tumult, much of it extant there in her trembling lines and not-square rectangles. A *dissonance* (Agnes's word) seems inherent, and this dissonance is actually a part of *recognizing your feelings at the same time*, if in fact the dissonance is not actually *a part of* the tranquility itself which, it must be noted, is made not born. This is emptiness and tranquility borne of effort, something the artist built, all while showing a great awareness that such trembling uncertainty is a given; perhaps happiness, so defined by Martin, includes inside itself an awareness of this difficulty, even the certainty of failure. Perhaps happiness, for Martin, is big enough to encompass those things. What if happiness is the bigger thing?

Inside this question, I'm suddenly afraid: I am not ready to admit to myself, as Martin has, that the purpose of art may be to unlock an inner happiness in the viewer. I am doubtful such a happiness is inherent, and unsure whether it is larger than forces with which I've engaged my own work (such as grief and difficulty). I am uncertain I can place the function of art, art-making, its practice, in the category of making-happy, given all I've seen and felt in the last five years, all my children have endured in the service of gaining a working understanding of the world into which they've been thrown. Of course, any difficulty can be a subset of happiness, Martin's work virtually shouts at me. Don't be so narrow-minded.

What Martin is asking of me as viewer, this particular level of emptiness, can be the work of a lifetime, hers, mine. We approach the work in order to empty ourselves as we acknowledge that work is ongoing.

Even with that knowledge, Martin can say: *And so I painted it and then I was satisfied.*

Ideas on Emptiness

In an interview, Martin refers to the emptiness this way: "I don't have any ideas myself. I have a vacant mind." Later she notes this vacant quality gives room for what she calls "inspiration" to arrive, after which a lot of work—years of work—is involved to begin to approach the quality she seeks in a painting, "scaling up" the postage-stamp image that appears to her. Instead of inspiration, I would call the idea for the painting a by-product of a deliberate and continually practiced devotion, and Martin might agree. "Every day for twenty years," she said, "I would say what am I going to do next. That's how I asked for inspiration."

Writing about another painter practiced in cultivating an abstract emptiness inside tumult, in his poem entitled "Vermeer," Tomas Tranströmer writes, "It hurts to go through walls, it makes you sick / but it's necessary." It's the going through walls—whether in Martin those walls are the emptiness of no idea, the time one sits waiting, the math one does to scale it, or the mistake of the pencil running crooked—that deepens joyful emotions, that creates the pastel quality that illuminates and complicates the word "innocence," much in the way a rectangle "destroys" a square. Earlier in the poem, the poet imagines Vermeer in his studio in Delft, "No sheltered world...on the other side of the wall

/ the noise begins / the tavern begins / with laughter and bickering, rows of teeth, tears / the din of bells..."

Laughter, bickering, rows of teeth, tears. Martin's life was no different; though her studio away from the "din" of New York City, in Cuba, then Galisteo, New Mexico, seems to have taken some of the noise out of the "other side of the wall," there is the din inside each of us to be stilled and mined as well. There is no such thing as a sheltered world, Martin well knew. Thus the reason for painting. The paintings ask us to find shelter inside ourselves, to allow the feelings that are already inside us to begin the work of creating—then disrupting, mindfully—a sense of an order. Let the dissonance in, Martin says, let it do its (happy) work.

At the end of "Vermeer," Tranströmer describes the "clear sky" in the painting as a "prayer to emptiness. / And the emptiness turns its face to us / and whispers, / 'I am not empty, I am open.'"

No Sheltered World

To see that one is not empty but open is the work of a lifetime. For reasons none of us have chosen, both of my boys have learned (in their own time and way) there is no shelter but their own. And I think they begin to see that the dissonance *within themselves* has work to do in their lives, that emptiness can become openness. And that art is here to help them. It hurts to go through walls, it makes you sick, but it's necessary.

Luke is practicing archery with a new bow, a trembling discovery of the last week or so, and to do so he must empty his mind as he aims. His eye follows the line the arrow makes as surely as Martin followed her straightedge, leading with satisfaction to the target, the canvas's end. He and his friends have dreams of hunting a hawk that has recently raided a robin's nest, taking its two chicks. After twenty or thirty tries, he hits the bullseye; the sound of that arrow made the same sound as all the other arrows that missed the home-made target, boxes piled one over the other to aria of stream, helicopter, and bowstring. Before he went down to practice, he stopped again to look at *Summer, 1964* and decided that he did feel *something*. He left without naming what the feeling was and instead took it down with him to practice.

On the video, Agnes is sharpening a pencil, saying that a painting made truly abstract corresponds to "a tremendous range of abstract feeling" inside each of us. Watching Luke aim empty I believe her. She is eighty-eight, no longer in her studio in Galisteo, where she had moved from Cuba in 1977, and where she made the paintings that comprise her distinctive late style, but in an assisted living facility where she continues to paint until she dies at the age of ninety-two. As she works, she remarks that the painting she is aiming for is "really abstract—without any cause in this world." Cause? No cause but its own complicated, hard-worn (and trembling) emptiness.

Martin sharpens her pencil in an old crank-handled sharpener, then sharpens it once more manually with the edge of the table, takes up her level, and begins.

TWO

Of Morning Glass: Becoming a Swimmer

Is this the first time that feeling comes, not at all frightening, but familiar to you? Your understanding of the water and its relation to the body, your being able to hold your own inside the enormous unimaginable, to dive deep and come up far from where you started: When does it begin? Is it the day you step off of the last step in the shallow end of a neighbor's pool up the street near the river, the water line shifting your vision to divide all that is in from all that is not in water? Or earlier, when you walk into the waves *out front*—an expression that means the water of the vast Atlantic Ocean that flows almost to your doorstep—feeling for the first time the relief that there is a thing that is much bigger than you, enormous in fact? Or the feeling has its roots in the way your father talks about the stars that make up the Milky Way, your relation to them mathematical, an infinite sense of connection among bodies, each floating in its atmosphere.

In reality *out front* is not at your doorstep but five hundred yards of steaming asphalt from the three-bedroom, two-bath bungalow in which your parents have raised seven children. You walk it blind, having learned the way of each and every pebble donated to the asphalt mix, and the pebbles in turn have learned the feel of your leathering skin. *Out front* beyond the cut-through, first through the dunes and later as trespass walking under the stilts of houses that block your cut-through over dwindling and eroded dunes.

Hide and seek suffers these erosions. Pickle under the streetlight. Kick-the-can through the back yards. Eroded too, the presence of so many people in the house: brothers and a sister who each leave you there. Then you leave them, your parents, there. The erosions of time follow.

In truth *out front* is also a piece of language, one of the first phrases you learn, an idiom you share with the two hundred people (an estimate) who know what it means: the patch of the Atlantic Ocean directly in front of 219 Robinson Road, the house with all the surf boards in the back room, the one where the rocket scientist and his wife and their five sons and two daughters live. Later, it will be the spot of beach in front of the house where the widow lives, boards still there if you want to paddle out *out front*, catch a *dawn patrol*, use all of it as an excuse to check on her. You are a son home for a quick visit, a nephew crashing in a back bedroom, a boy who knew her daughter, a friend of someone who loved someone who lived here.

By the time you are writing this the very house you ran home to as the rain followed you in sheets from the beach is not gone but gutted, remodeled. Whoever remodeled it has not changed the pitch of the roof, and as you walk barefoot from *out front* down the street you recognize that pitch. Like a music it sings to you.

Out front is two hundred yards of beach in front of a side street on a barrier island seventeen miles long and half a mile wide. Driving, take the south causeway to reach it, if you are worried the draw bridge on the north causeway will stop you. Swimming from Crawford Approach, the Atlantic's northerly current takes you quickly past it. Blink and you're halfway to the inlet, already approaching Beachway. You'll have a long walk back.

⚓

Though *out front* is simply the ocean in front of a phantom house, these decades later you still have the habitual stroke that you developed there. Rarely do you have an expanse of water big enough to use it. Its memory dwarfs a house pool, makes you restless in the lap pools of several towns in which you settle: Poughkeepsie, Amherst, Northampton, Gloucester, Charleston, Newtown. You try out YMCA's, high-school and university pools, community centers, but you are meant for salt water. And anyway yours is a distance-swimmer's stroke, three pulls with each arm (six total) before you take a breath on your left side. This gets you two-thirds of the way down an olympic-sized pool before you begin your flip-turn. In the ocean, you can get about three hundred yards out with about ten of these. You like to get far enough out that the curve of the earth hides the beach. Counting is important without the end of the pool to keep track of lengths. In the ocean you swim out until the beach disappears, then over. From Flagler to *out front,* depending on the current, is about eighty breaths. The lifeguards know you can handle yourself far out so they don't call you back. They also know how deep it is out there and know you know it, too.

The habitual stroke gives you swimmer's ear and more muscle tone on one side—an imbalance and a strength. You should breathe on both sides, you should alternate this stroke, but you don't ever do it. Anyway, you much prefer diving far down in the water and swimming for as long as you can before you pop back up, but this is something the lifeguards would worry after. It would distract them from the possible drownings right under their noses, the ones involving those overcome by the surf, to keep track of where you disappear and resurface. The line of surf is a game to you—when a wave is too big for you to jump over you are deep under it before it can get you—it's a slight pull at your back as you shine yourself out the other side and begin with those habitual pulls to head deeper, farther. Your brothers are surfing out front and you want to meet them. Or if not your brothers, their friends, and if not them, your nephews, or your nephews' friends, all of them at least once have stored a board at the phantom house, have slipped in while your mother is taking her afternoon nap, checked her breathing.

The edge of the continent outside her door, and for many years, yours. Any time of day you can come here and walk it. Some days you swim but other days you walk two miles at a stretch feeling the way in which the outgoing tide has shaped and reshaped the surface of the hard sand into ridges, a river bed, a pillowy mattress with pockets of air left when the water lava'd its way over mounds of dry sand, trapping air particles, then receded. You like to walk blind on solitary days and feel the sense of your feet touching so many millions of particles of sand, some of them surface dwellers, others churned-up new arrivals. And you come here after storms for the shells, mounds of them in jars and tupperware in your room in the house down the street. From there you can lie in bed and listen hard to know what the waves are doing, whether out front is glassy or choppy. Or someone in your house will have already checked the waves before you woke up, will have headed out front to surf. Before you wake up you will have registered this, it will pull you from sleep the way the tide pulls itself out; you will slip on a suit to go find your brother surfing, or his friend, one of whom has snuck into the back room (the board room but also your bedroom) and slipped out the side door with his board. You are such a good swimmer you find them easily and swim out to them, even on the outside break. Even on big days. Sometimes you say hi and swim out past them. No one gives you swimming this way a second thought.

※

It is much later when you find a name for it, oceanic, talking to a Roman Catholic priest at work, who says that the feeling-small-near-the-ocean feeling, the I'm-small-it's-big comfort that throughout your childhood you used to navigate the stripped, chaotic, unbound world, is a specific religious phenomenon common to many cultures. First described as *oceanic* by a correspondent of Freud's, the *oceanic feeling* is a specific sensation. Romain Rolland, after a meeting with Freud, wrote to him (in rough translation):

> But I would have liked to see you doing an analysis of *spontaneous religious sentiment* or, more exactly, of religious *feeling*, which is…the simple and direct fact *of the feeling of the "eternal"* (which can very well not be eternal, but simply without perceptible limits, and like oceanic, as it were).

A *feeling of the "eternal"*: the water over your head, you holding strong under the upward pull of the wave, something innate or learned—how can you tell now—about how to dive first and then resist the pull of the building wave wall that has already broken on top of you, is moving away from your body as you swim powerfully out of its grasp. Your habit of no fear, your going out far, farther than most. The sense that tired just means float, rest. Then swim more. As if you are in your element. *Simply without perceptible limits*: you could, if you chose to, swim for hours directly away from the coast. That a limit is not perceptible does not mean you will not reach yours suddenly, an end to your reserves. You are not sure where that end point is because you have not met it. Your impulse seems to be a willingness to dive deep, to partake in *spontaneous religious sentiment*. A simple and direct fact of your way of being that the ocean, in its scale and beauty, seems to answer.

You've been told the continental shelf is closer here, on this beach, than any other point in the eastern Atlantic shoreline, and that explains the strange sea creatures that wash up, the mile-long worms and large grey egg sacks (underwater cliff-dwellers shored by storms). You've been told the larger marine animals swim closer to shore here. You have not reached them on your limitless swims, but you sense they are there.

You are no more than eight years old and as many as twenty when you ritually swim like this. You are accompanied by the musculature of your arms and legs, the beating of your strong heart, and the oceanic feeling.

⁂

When your father talks about the stars and your relation to them you listen. Perhaps this is because he has calculated the route the astronauts have taken to the moon, has returned them on their perilous return to the earth when it no longer seemed they could make it. You imagine he has done these enormous actions the way he has tucked you into bed, with a matter-of-fact, competent kindness.

You also listen because the sky belongs to you and him. Your first memories of this sky, some of the first times you heard the ocean the way you always hear it now, you laid in an old-fashioned perambulator your father would wheel down to the beach at night. He would walk you along this edge you've grown so attached to, looking up at the stars. Perhaps he was thinking of the names of the astronauts he'd placed there and returned, or the ones who burned up on the pad. That first Apollo mission would haunt him even though the rest came back. For years the rest would come back, for most of your childhood the sound of these waves and your father coming and going from NASA.

A feeling of the eternal…mostly without perceptible limits. You both had insomnia, he said. So he took you with him on these sky-edged walks.

꙳

You are in high school when you mind the radio in the tower at Flagler Approach that has a view of the boys with the flags at each lifeguard tower for six miles, thirty of them altogether, including the ones that come to visit you, the lunch relays, who give the tower guards lunch but otherwise lounge with you four stories up in your radio booth, where you take the binoculars and look, count eight, ten flags till you lose sight of the far ones to the curve of the beach and the haze in the air. If they have a rescue they're to tell you on the radio, but if they have to go quickly because someone is drowning they can simply drop their flag and run. Every other guard will drop his flag until the relay reaches you. So you watch the farthest flag you can see while you listen to the dispatch radio. You don't look up or away when the lunch relay climbs your stairs, a sensation that shakes the tower with each step. When he arrives you are looking straight out into the blue. Of course you do stop looking through your binoculars to talk with him, but not right away. This is serious work.

There are one or two tower guards who are girls among so many boys, but in the station you are a girl among men; you on the radio, the one they hear, the one they tease, clicking their radios in their boredom, asking you the time of day, or the time of high tide or low. Each of them, like you, has grown up on this beach and the timetable of tides is so ingrained they can tell high or low from their beds, from the way the air smells or the wind stops as the tide turns, but they like hearing your voice. You are quick and reassuring and familiar, your voice low and steady. They like to ask you questions you have to answer in front of everyone. None of it goes very far.

You are also the one who quiets them when a rescue is underway, saying 10-63 which means only emergency communications while the officers (the men, their supervisors, who mostly sit around in the downstairs station refusing you your bathroom break, your lunch break) head off with lights and sirens in their truck (called the unit, another joke word you say over radio twitters and clicks) to the tower (numbered sequentially south to north, 602 to 640) that has the rescue. In this manner you oversee the silence of many rescues, most only a few minutes long. Certain tower numbers—636, 618, 602—you listen archly for during rescues, aware from your own swimming they are dangerous spots for their run-out currents or steep drop offs. And you listen for 640, the northernmost tower on your beach, the one edged by the inlet that separates your beach from the next town over, in case sharks have come south from the north side of the inlet into the surfing area. But shark attacks are uncommon.

In this manner, over the several summers it takes you to graduate high school, college, then graduate school, you are the dispatcher on a few near-drownings, the silence growing longer till your captain tells you to call an ambulance or that a family has transported the victim in their own vehicle to the hospital. No more than once or twice, you preside over the extended silence of an actual drowning, the captain calling for an ambulance to come and wait while he, the tower guard, every officer, and every available lunch relay, converges on the scene to dead man dive into the water at the body's last known location, searching for the body with their every extremity, spread out like starfish, until they find the body or the time has passed when the brain could survive without oxygen, a complicated calculation that requires the captain to ask you on air for the water temperature and time of rescue. You provide it, briefly breaking the silence. While the captain does the math, the radio sleeps, sometimes for longer than the calculation required, because it's a hard thing for a group of swimmers to stop looking for a body in water.

While this is happening, you are looking far out where the ocean's depth changes the water's color, watching the shadows the clouds make on the surface of this infinite thing, so large now it is capable of swallowing swimmers whole. Your limbs itch to swim to where the deeper water is making its deeper blue. But you are at your binoculars trying to see down to where the unit has pulled up to the tower, where the ambulance waits, its lights off. Before you hear him you see the captain head to the unit to radio you. A series of numerical codes tells you and every listening guard that the radio is free now for normal use. Through the binoculars you see the tower guard climb back up to his position on the tower. It's him or, you can't tell which, maybe one of the lunch relays climbs up to finish the guard's shift. Someone—the lunch relays and tower guards are all boys of similar age so you can't tell—climbs into the back of the unit and heads back your way. Soon whoever that is will climb your stairs to tell you what has happened. But you are a swimmer yourself and you already know.

You swam drill with each one of them that morning, more than thirty of you swimming first 300 yards out, then 300 over, last 300 in, then jogging the three football fields back to the station. A 1,200 yard box, the perfect asymmetry of three parts sea, one part land. You don't have to swim with them—you're not a guard—but you do. You share as much of it as you can with them, knowing at some point a moment like this one is coming no one can share. Before anyone can climb up to tell you *the whole story*—while the

131

unit makes its slow way to you down the beach—you think of the difference between drowned and saved. You think how *story* is the wrong word for what the boy will come and tell you. And you think how you want to swim with all of them right now. You want to see their strong strokes ahead of you, then behind—you are a distance swimmer, suited to depths, and they are trained to sprint. Something in you wants to get into the water right away.

After work some of you paddle out on the rescue boards quiet, letting your muscles move in reassuring repetition. You take turns catching languorous sunset waves. You catch one wave with Lyle, a lunch relay who is an old friend of yours all the way back to Coronado Elementary. The both of you easily paddle in tandem on one long board, Lyle behind you in front, timing it so you stand together and ride the wave all the way in. No one says much. For a long time no one wants to go home—before you there seem to be several hours of this dusky glass to which each of you has been born.

⚓

You are grown and landlocked, living in Connecticut, when your older boy is at school one day and the news comes (on *the news*) that in your town, there's been a shooting. Long seconds pass before you find out it's not your boy's school but another, one school over from his. It's a half hour before you learn the extent of it: twenty first graders and six teachers are dead two miles from your son's school, even closer as the crow flies to your husband and your younger son, both home. Your husband is texting you what he can find out by looking at news online. He doesn't turn on the television news where Luke, your younger boy not at school because afternoon kindergarten is cancelled, might see it.

As you drive to pick up Willem, your older son, you can't shake the urge to swim, the resemblance of those seconds of waiting to radio silence. As soon as you are in the car with him you tell him what's happened and he asks to go home so you do. You do go home. What you want to do is swim out front. But what is *out front* to your boys? What are they born to as you were that water?

For weeks you wake to the sensation of gulping for air. You aim yourself, your sons, your husband, toward some kind of steady stroke. But swimming is a metaphor for something else. You replace *drowned* and *saved* with new words: *taken, not taken*. You learn all this but it will be years until you know it. You have to swim with it to take it into your body.

Years pass and the sensation that you are swimming a long way in deep water does not leave you. You become aware that this is simply a way of thinking about something you can't otherwise accommodate. When you are tired of swimming you float on its infinite surface, and you are not sure why but its infinite surface doesn't swallow you. Sometimes the codes and language of that time on the beach return to you: drownings, near-drownings. Sometimes you are swimming again with those morning guards. You see their young faces as they finish the box and barrel out of the water, and you see how they looked later, after they'd sat through all that radio silence.

꙳

But there are months in Newtown when your ears don't fill with water even once. One summer Luke, your younger boy, now ten, teaches himself to dive at the town pool. You see he is a natural in the water but you don't tell him what a swimmer you are. He swims the length of the pool in one breath and you wonder if some of it is genetic, innate. He has not grown up out front, next to the infinite feeling, yet somehow it's in his lungs. Or something in his own experience—the shooting, its aftermath—gives him a sense of living on the edge of a great depth. Not the edge of a continent, as you had, but the edge, perhaps, of what can be understood.

You were just a year or so older than him when you quit surfing. You remember the day partly because a storm had thrown up deep-water creatures (the white husks of long sea worms, malformed shells resembling the burls of sick trees) from the continental shelf. The water was still choppy. It was the fall, windy, already the beach was clear of tourists. All the lifeguard towers were moved up to the soft sand for the winter, which meant no guards even worked weekends anymore. Sometime after Columbus Day: October, your favorite, but once you were paddling out you saw the waves were bigger than you'd thought. It took you a long time to paddle out to the outside break as the lips of waves caught and pulled your board back. But you made it.

This was a short board, handed down by a brother to you, and to ride for any length of time you had to turn and ride the face of the wave, gathering the speed for the short board from the froth that followed it. Until that day you hadn't been able to turn this way, but that day, something in you figures it out. You don't figure it out so much as begin to use your swimmer's mind. As it does your steady stroke your body makes the turn. Later you won't be able to recreate how. You will just know it is the first and last time you will do it. You'll remember as you paddled out thinking how much stronger you'd be against all this water with just your body rather than this clumsy board—too buoyant to take with you on your long dives under the waves, it always dragged you backwards into the froth. The way a surface thought prevents its deeper imagining, maybe. Or how a child is called to dinner away from the possibility of play.

Maybe the heaviness of the board persuades you to give it up. After that in the water you were always swimming. As Luke dives and swims to the limit of his breath, you don't tell him any of this and you quit thinking of it as quitting surfing. Rather, you chose swimming. You don't ask what Luke is quitting, what he's choosing to take with him into his muscle memory. Maybe he won't feel he has to choose.

What is the relationship of a vessel to what it holds? You are aware of the relationship of your skin to the blood, the organs, the bones and joints it holds in place. You have some sense of it from church, too—*Make of me a vessel of your peace.* And from the coastline, a sense of the shifting but mathematically predictable way in which high tide follows low every six hours plus twenty minutes, something you can calculate two weeks out, the amount of time it takes the world to turn upside down from high to low. The tides a kind of vessel in which the ocean is kept. But you know rogue waves and tides disrupt it, take a bite out of the coastline or sweep a child out to sea. You know because you have seen both happen.

While you swim you are a vessel for what you hold, and also part of what is held. This is the key to the oceanic feeling. In the months after the shooting all you want is to feel again this floating oceanic certainty you felt as a child, but vessels have been breached everywhere. All over town vessels are spilling. You pull and breathe and flip-turn in pools that are too small for what your body now knows, what it has been asked to take in.

You know though you are not bone-familiar with it that there is a point inland where the tide no longer has any pull, and the water there seems ruled by something besides the cosmos. You find it strange that this water that has no relation to the moon is called *fresh*. On the vessel that holds that water you are not well versed but you wonder if this is part of living with the shooting—the vessel and what holds it reversing themselves, the cosmos, its order, no longer available to turn the system back to a tidal kind of order. No flip-turn in fresh water will help you.

It will be six years since the shooting before you swim in big enough salt water, water different enough from your childhood, to mark any kind of reordering. You are not sure if you can return to *a feeling of the eternal*, but you swim anyway. It's north of Barcelona, at a small rocky beach called Aiguablava, where you and the boys and your husband climb the rock ledge that leads to the next beach over, having heard there is a spot where you can swim in an infinity pool made by these rock formations. Online the pictures seem color-altered, but when you get to the coastline you see it really *is* this impossible shade of blue. When you get to the place in the rocks where there should be a pool, you realize the pool appears only at high tide and you have come at low tide. The fishermen below you know the tide tables but you do not. This is not your ocean. You have not taken note of the tide at your arrival at the beach—the amnesia of a muscle left neglected these landlocked years—and now there is only sweat and disappointment. You scan the rocks for a safe place to enter the larger sea (rather than a small protected pool). Your body tells you that you can swim all the way back to Aiguablava and that swimming is better than the long rocky staircase you've climbed to reach it. And your body wants the open water.

The boys, eleven and fifteen now, want to go with you, if you can find the place where the waves won't dash you each on the rocks, the sweet spot where the current won't send you far out from the coast. Your husband notices a series of buoys that line the coast of the two beaches, indicating others have swum the route, and agrees you all can swim back. He will carry your things and watch you from the high path.

Painstakingly and not without some slips (the rocks are covered with moss at low tide) you find a covelet where the current runs out but not too far, just enough to clear the rocks. You will jump in first—waiting till the waves are between *sets* (a word you remember from surfing, the number of waves that come before a minutes-long rest), showing the boys how to jump out and away from the rocks to the deepest part of the small channel. You jump out and you are in, underwater. Both ears fill and the sound you hear is the economy of so much water, its negotiation with the rocks. Then you surface and hold out your hands for Luke next, then Willem.

All three of you are swimming now. Almost immediately you feel vessel-in-vessel, the oceanic feeling. You watch your boys and think: *There is something to doing again in adulthood what you learned to do when you were very young.* As soon as you think it you leave the thought, positioning yourself behind your sons so they are in your sight always.

A few strokes later you are all safely away from the coast. You spot your husband high up on the cliff, and finding the three of you he takes a picture. Later you are three almost imperceptible specks in an impossible blue enormity. It's the oceanic feeling, the boys safe inside it, something you've rarely felt for them on land. And you are aware that what you once held has spilled out into the world.

You meet this knowledge with your strong stroke, your steady beating heart. You let yourself be what is held and its vessel. You swim as you empty, and you empty as you swim.

⁂

You are back from that new water, back in Newtown, when you watch Luke diving by rote. Not into water this time but into the flat unforgiving ground, toward a ball, over and over, in goalie practice. A game of cosmic pong, his body the paddle sent in one direction, then the other. Later he tells you there was a pebble in the grass. He did his best to time his dive to avoid it. He gives you a quick glance at the sharp lines his body made grazing it, not cuts but welts. You recall swimming the opposite way through a school of fish on a morning drill, the fish so strong and—surprised?—slapping against your body. No cuts but marks on your body after. And you think of timing your dives under the biggest waves.

Again you think of the silence on the radio, your order 10-63 to quiet the tower guards, this time because a boy not much older than you, a guard from Dunlawton station north of your inlet, the next town over, is narrating something he sees near the inlet, on the north side of the rocks that divide your town from his. In fact, he is so far south you can probably hear him better than his home dispatcher, the signal strong to you, but he is talking to another girl like you ten miles north as the pelicans fly from your position. He is telling her that some men—or boys—he can't tell—have pulled a sea turtle out of the surf three hundred yards from his tower and are butchering it with a machete. He is asking permission to go stop them and she is telling him she has called the police, that he has no weapon to take them on, that theirs is a federal offense and they will be arrested. He answers back that he has the hard side of his buoy. In his voice is a cry for all the beauty that he has taken into his body living on this beach, all the tidal shifts, every swim he has ever taken. You take out your binoculars to see if you can see into the no-man's-land between your two beaches, a stretch between two identical jetties, where the boy says the men are, but it's too far. You can't ask 640 what he sees because you're on radio silence. That silence yawns while the dispatcher asks the captain his permission for the guard to go and he refuses, then a moment later the captain reports he is on the way to the location (the 10-20), then nothing.

In a little while the airwaves open again to normal traffic. You don't find out what happened exactly but you can imagine. Into your swimmer's body you have taken two drownings and a turtle butchering and you are not yet twenty.

On the pitch Luke is diving one way then the other. His coach sends the second ball before the first ball is fully repelled, a speeded-up pong. He catches more at more impossible angles. Out of the corner of his eye an imaginary school of fish, swimming in his direction, changes course with him, lifting him above all that might scratch him.

⚹

You return from your swim in the Mediterranean to the twelfth-century castle with five guest rooms. Every morning its devoted owner has served you a cake you guess is a pilgrim's cake, eaten for centuries as pilgrims walk this way toward the Pyrenees. Almonds, no wheat flour. His English is spotty, your Spanish nonexistent, but he tells you. When you ask about the dog, he tells you his name is Fosc, the Catalan word for *dark*, and complains that everyone loves the dog. No one comments on the painstaking renovation of the 800-year old building, but the dog they love. Everyone loves the dark, he says.

There is no darkness in this dog—a big gold king of a German Shepherd—but the owner tells me before this dog he had a black dog who died. Afterwards he got this dog and named it Fosc for the dog that is gone. You tell him your boys have come up with a theory that Fosc is beloved because Fosc has been here for 800 years, *dark* is every dog who has ever lived here, which makes the man who mourns a dead dog smile.

Perhaps this exchange is why he stops you as you come in from your beach-to-beach low-tide swim. Fosc's man has been mowing in Fosc's hay fields. The man opens his hand to show you a small thing in his large palm. He has found what you first think is a smooth pebble, grey as a sky over morning glass. Then he shows you its unbroken side. A stone? You say, and he shakes his head. Fosc has come to see what the matter is. With a twist of his wrist your innkeeper turns the stone over and shows you its tiny hole: it's an egg from the swallow's nest above, saved from the mower by his keen eye. He hands it to you, a vessel that kept a chick floating all those warm nights, now empty. You bring it across an ocean, taking care to wrap it in a glasses' case and paper, and it sits on a blue saucer on your writing desk. It *swims* there, swims as Fosc swims through centuries bearing the name of all other dogs, substance and vessel both.

⁂

Earlier on this same trip you and Willem had been out at dusk in a small town in France. One night driving back to the house you've rented you see a herd of goats and sheep, dogs tending them, and their man walking behind. When you reach the house your husband and Luke head inside but you and Willem follow the sound of the bells back down to see if you can catch them before they leave the field. There, in the dusk, do you find them eating grass. If you get too close they startle, so you back up. Soon the oceanic feeling comes: the sound of the bells, the line of horizon, a salty dusk.

You have been to this town once before, pregnant. The last time you were here, he, now taller than you, floated six weeks in a pool of amniotic fluid inside you. This light at dusk, these same fields, your two bodies several now. You realize you've taken him back to the place of his becoming without intending to, without knowing until this moment that you were doing it.

Willem takes your head onto his shoulder to fit you into the frame of his selfie. He pushes your head gently up with his free hand and it stays here, his hand on your head. You realize you can float inside almost anything. Something lifts you from underneath. You can be the thing inside the vessel and someone else, your own son, can be the vessel that holds it, opposite of when you were last here.

※

Morning glass starts as a feeling under the sheet on your skin before you open your eyes. You know this feeling at eight and ten. At twenty and forty it is still recognizable.

A lot changes but this doesn't: a quality of no wind. You slip on your clothes—while you do so you return from the nakedness of sleep into the quicksilver of thought. If you don't find something to put on your feet you go barefoot. You walk toward the end of the street where you already know the water is glassy: because of no wind, because of the blinding heat, because of where the tide was the last time you turned your head toward the ocean on your way home.

As natural as the last time you checked the thing inside you that beats such a steady rhythm, noting in it waves, small or large and steady in your chest.

Because they are not yet eroded to nothing, you walk through the hot dunes until your thighs burn. Finally you see it: a silver sheet of gelatin. The waves that come don't break so much as fold noiselessly back into the calm surface of their making. Doing so they form a perfect shape. During the long hot day you know the morning glass will disappear and the waves will lose their definition. But for now there is quiet and perfection and the possibility that you are part of it.

You walk slowly out. Your body in this water approximates the nakedness of sleep. Waist deep, then chest deep. Then you are swimming, the rhythmic, familiar pull of the body by the arms. The water, too glassy to resist you, holds you up and moves you quickly far out. Like the waves your movements don't disrupt its surface. You say hello to the thing inside you that beats its steady hum. You are a small thing floating on the surface of morning glass.

NOTES

This book's epigraph is a passage from Walt Whitman's "A child said, What is the grass?" First published in the 1855 edition of *Leaves of Grass*.

The following works instrumental to my thinking and writing are listed by the essay in which the resource was especially important, given in the order to which they are referred within the essay.

THE ONE I GET AND OTHER ARTIFACTS

Elizabeth Bishop. Excerpt from "Under the Window: Ouro Preto," from *The Complete Poems 1927–1979*. Farrar, Straus and Giroux, 1983.

BEFORE I GET TO MY DESK

Miklós Radnóti. *All That Still Matters at All: Selected Poems of Miklós Radnóti*. Translated by John M. Ridland and Peter Czipott. New American Press, 2014.

Miklós Radnóti. "Forced March," from *Clouded Sky*, translated by Steven Polgar, Stephen Berg, and S. J. Marks. Sheep Meadow Press, 2003.

Hélène Cixous. *Stigmata*. Particularly passages from the essays "Bathsheba or the Interior Bible" and "What Is It O'Clock? Or the Door (We Never Enter)," translated by Catherine A. F. MacGillivray. Routledge Classics, 1998.

THE PRACTICE OF SCHOOL BUSSES AND HUMMINGBIRDS

Jalal al-Din Rumi. *Mystical Poems of Rumi, First Selection: Poems 1–200*. Most quotations are from poems 84 and 105.Translated by A. J. Arberry. University of Chicago Press, 1968.

Larry Levis. *The Gazer Within*. University of Michigan Press, 2001.

Ivan Bunin. "The Scent of Apples," from *Collected Stories of Ivan Bunin*. Translated by Graham Hettlinger. Ivan R. Dee, 2007.

MEMOIR OF SLEEP AND WAKING

Eva Hesse. *Datebooks, 1964/65 A Facsimile Edition*. Yale University Press, 2006.

Eva Hesse. Edited by Mignon Nixon. MIT Press, 2002.

The Papers of the Helen and Eva Hesse Family, 1882–1956. Leo Baeck Institute, Center for Jewish History, accessed online.

ON BROTHERHOOD AND CRUCIFIXION

Simone Wiel. *Waiting for God*. Translated by Emma Craufurd. Putnam, 1951.

Mark Thompson. *American Character: The Curious Life of Charles Fletcher Lummis and the Rediscovery of the Southwest.* Arcade, 2001.

LOOSE THREAD

Paul Celan. "I hear the axe has flowered." Translated by Ian Fairley, from *Snow Part / Schneepart* (Sheep Meadow Press, 2007).

Paul Celan. "Deathfugue." Translated by John Felstiner, from *Selected Poems and Prose of Paul Celan.* Norton, 2000.

Arshile Gorky: A Retrospective. Including the essay by Kim Servart Theriault on "The Artist and His Mother." Edited by Michael R. Taylor. Philadelphia Museum of Art / Yale University Press, 2009.

Hayden Herrera. *Arshile Gorky: His Life and Work.* Farrar, Straus and Giroux, 2003.

Matthew Spender. *From a High Place: A Life of Arshile Gorky.* Knopf, 1999.

A COVERING SNOW

Picasso Sculpture. Edited by Ann Temkin and Anne Umland. Museum of Modern Art, 2015.

Hélène Cixous. *Stigmata.* Translated by Catherine A. F. MacGillivray, et al. Routledge Classics, 1998.

Guillaume Apollinaire. "Il pleut." Translated by Roger Shattuck, from *Selected Writings of Guillaume Apollinaire.* New Directions, 1971.

Edward Hirsch. "Winged Type," from *How to Read a Poem: And Fall in Love with Poetry*. Harcourt, 1999. This essay about Apollinaire was republished on the website of the Poetry Foundation, including a reproduction of the poem "Il pleut" in its original graphic format.

No Sheltered World

Agnes Martin. Edited by Frances Morris and Tiffany Bell. Distributed Art Publishers / Tate Modern, 2015.

Arne Glimcher. *Agnes Martin: Paintings, Writings, Remembrances*. Phaidon Press, 2012.

Donald Woodman. *Agnes Martin and Me*. Lyon Artbooks, 2016.

Dean Young. *The Art of Recklessness: Poetry as Assertive Force and Contradiction*. Graywolf Press, 2010.

Tomas Tranströmer. "Vermeer." Translated and copyright © 1987 Samuel Charters, from *Selected Poems 1954–1986*. Edited by Robert Hass. Ecco, 1987.

Gratitude is also expressed to the museums whose halls I have wandered to experience firsthand many of the artworks discussed: The Aldrich Contemporary Art Museum, The Museum of Modern Art, The Solomon R. Guggenheim Museum, and the Yale University Art Gallery.

ACKNOWLEDGMENTS

I thank all who contribute to Tupelo Press, in particular Jeffrey Levine, Jim Schley, and David Rossitter, without whom these words are writ on water.

I am grateful to the editors of publications in which many of these essays (some with different titles) originally appeared: *Agni, American Poetry Review, The Georgia Review*, and *Image*. Gratitude is expressed to participants on juries who singled out those essays for additional notice subsequent to their journal publication: "The One I Get and Other Artifacts" as one of five finalists for the National Magazine Award in the Essays and Criticism category and for a Pushcart Prize Special Mention; "The Practice of School Busses and Hummingbirds," "Memoir of Sleep and Waking," "A Covering Snow," and "Loose Thread" as Notable in the *Best American Essays* series.

As this book was being prepared for press, news came of the death of my classmate, the poet and lyricist David C. Berman. I acknowledge in this space my gratitude for his deep humanity and for his friendship.

My friends in Newtown renew me each day with their common devotion to what Rumi might call the work of our "ongoing wholeness." Susan, Matt, Nancy, Dione, Tracey, Theresa, Lea, Cindy, Joanna, Lakhdar, Mark, Amy, Chris, Monica, Carla, Elaine, Kate, Twyla, Priscilla, Paula, Francine and many others knit me together at bus stops, on playing fields, at concerts, at poetry workshops, and in praying moments. I thank each of you for the grace of your daily presence in my life.

For the ways each has seen and cared for me during these years at Fairfield University, I thank Beth Boquet, Betsy Bowen, Lindy Briggette, Bryan Crandall, David Crawford, Michael DeStefano, Thomas Fitzpatrick, Johanna Garvey, Richard Greenwald, Kim Gunter, Sonya Huber, William Johnson, Paul Lakeland, Margaret McClure, Linda Miller, Karen Osborn, Elizabeth Petrino, Melissa Quan, Jay Rozgonyi, Kris Sealey, Christine Siegel, Emily Smith, and Tiffany Wilgar. Likewise, for my years at The College of Charleston, I remain grateful to Paul Allen, Jennifer Baker, Lynne Ford, Margaret Hagood, Jonathan Ray, Theresa Owens, and Marjory Wentworth. A special thanks to my students, who buoy me and expand my thinking in crucial aspects.

To those who continue to teach in Newtown and in so many other towns affected by gun violence, thank you for the ongoing nature of your commitment, and for your courage.

My mother died before the publication of this book but lived through that terrible day with us; her care to her grandsons and me during its years-long aftermath remains a model of filial abidance.

My siblings striate these pages with their own dazzling complexities. Then as now love brought them to me and love is all that is left of them who made us.

ʎ

Finally, Garrett, Willem, and Luke: you are all and everything always.

CAROL ANN DAVIS is a poet, essayist, and author of the poetry collections *Psalm* (2007) and *Atlas Hour* (2011), both from Tupelo Press. The daughter of one of the NASA engineers who returned the Apollo 13 crew from the moon, she grew up on the east coast of Florida the youngest of seven children, then studied poetry at Vassar College and the University of Massachusetts, Amherst. A former longtime editor of the literary journal *Crazyhorse,* she is Professor of English at Fairfield University, where she is founding director of Poetry in Communities, an initiative that brings writing workshops to communities hit by sudden or systemic violence. She lives in Newtown, Connecticut, with her husband and two sons.

Recent and Selected Titles from Tupelo Press

See our complete list at tupelopress.org